MAGIC IN THE ROMAN WORLD

This volume demonstrates that the word "magic" was widely employed in late antique texts as part of polemical attacks on enemies – but at the simplest level it was merely a term used for other people's rituals.

The study begins by analysing Jewish, Christian and Greco-Roman uses of the term in the first three centuries CE. The author then turns to a series of in-depth examples of "magical" practice – exorcisms, love rites, alchemy and the transformation of humans into divine beings – examining how such rituals were thought to work. The book ends with an exploration of issues of gender and magic, looking at the reasons behind the over-representation of women on charges of using magic.

Janowitz's lively and accessible work illuminates the fact that activities denounced as magical were integral to late antique religious practice, and shows that they must be understood from the perspective of those who employed them.

Naomi Janowitz is Associate Professor of Religious Studies at the University of California-Davis. She is the author of *Poetics of Ascent* (1989) and numerous articles on the religions of late antiquity.

RELIGION IN THE FIRST CHRISTIAN CENTURIES

Edited by Deborah Sawyer and John Sawyer,
Lancaster University

The aim of the books in this series is to survey particular themes in the history of religion across the different religions of antiquity and to set up comparisons and contrasts, resonances and discontinuities, and thus reach a profounder understanding of the religious experience in the ancient world.

Also available in this series:

WOMEN AND RELIGION IN THE FIRST CHRISTIAN CENTURIES
Deborah F. Sawyer

THE CRUCIBLE OF CHRISTIAN MORALITY
J. Ian H. McDonald

SACRED LANGUAGES AND SACRED TEXTS
John Sawyer

DEATH, BURIAL AND REBIRTH IN THE RELIGIONS OF ANTIQUITY
Jon Davies

TEACHERS AND TEXTS IN THE ANCIENT WORLD: PHILOSOPHERS, JEWS AND CHRISTIANS
H. Gregory Snyder

HOLINESS: RABBINIC JUDAISM AND THE GRAECO-ROMAN WORLD
Hannah K. Harrington

MAGIC IN THE ROMAN WORLD

Pagans, Jews and Christians

Naomi Janowitz

London and New York

First published 2001
by Routledge
11 New Fetter Lane, London EC4P 4EE

Simultaneously published in the USA and Canada
by Routledge
29 West 35th Street, New York, NY 10001

Routledge is an imprint of the Taylor & Francis Group

Typeset in Garamond by Exe Valley Dataset Ltd, Exeter
Printed and bound in Great Britain by
T J International Ltd, Padstow, Cornwall

British Library Cataloguing in Publication Data
A catalogue record for this book is available from the British Library

Library of Congress Cataloging in Publication Data
Janowitz, Naomi
Magic in the Roman World; pagans, Jews, and Christians/Naomi Janowitz.
p. cm. – (Religion in the first Christian centuries)
Includes bibliographical references and index.
1. Magic, Ancient. 2. Rites and ceremonies–History. I. Title. II. Series.
BF1591.J36 2001
133.4309015–dc21

ISBN 0–415–20207–8 (pbk)
ISBN 0–415–20206–X (hbk)

For Rebecca

CONTENTS

PREFACE

When I was asked to write a book on magic in the first three centuries I was not sure how to proceed, since, as the reader will discover, this in my view is not a coherent topic. The result before you, a short introduction to a bewildering topic, could be called "The Artifice of Magic." It begins with a review of the workmanship that went into ancient notions of "magic," and includes some comments on modern artifice as well. In the subsequent chapters I ask the reader to explore a variety of once-maligned rituals without using the word "magic." Readers may wish to read the more technical discussion of some of these rituals included in my book *Icons of Power: The Pragmatics of Late Antique Ritual*, forthcoming from Penn State Press.

Numerous teachers and students have helped me think over ancient texts and modern methods, far too many to name. In particular the students in my graduate seminar at Hebrew University read and commented on various drafts and their enthusiasm was critical to finishing the project.

Additional guidance came from the participants and audiences at the symposium "Magic and Witchcraft in the Ancient, Medieval and Renaissance Worlds" at the UCLA Center for the Study of Women and at conferences in Israel organized by Moshe Idel, Ithamar Gruenwald, Yuval Harrari and Michael Mach.

I want especially to thank John Sawyer, editor for the series *The First Christian Centuries*, and Richard Stoneman at Routledge for many good suggestions and for their patience. Technical questions were answered by Tal Ilan, Brian Schmidt, and David Olster. Editorial help came from Patricia Stuckey, Devorah Schoenfeld and Andrew Lazarus. University of California Davis Research Grants supported the work.

ABBREVIATIONS

Rabbinic	(m=Mishnah, j=Jerusalem Talmud, b=Babylonian Talmud, t=tosefta
AZ	Avodah Zara
BabaB	Baba Batra
BabaK	Baba Kamma
Erub	Erubin
EsthRab	Esther Rabbah
GenRab	Genesis Rabbah
Git	Gittin
Hag	Hagigah
Hul	Hullin
Ket	Ketubot
Kid	Kiddushin
LamRab	Lamentations Rabbah
LevRab	Leviticus Rabbah
Meg	Megilla
Meil	Meila
Nid	Niddah
Pes	Pesachim
Pesiq Rab Kah	Pesiqta dRab Kahana
PesRab	Pesiqte Rabbati
Pirqe R El	Pirqe dRabbi Eleazar
RH	Rosh Hashanah
Sanh	Sanhedrin
Shab	Shabbat
Shev	Shevuot
ShirRab	Songs of Songs Rabbah
Suc	Succah
Yeb	Yebamot

Greco-Roman Sources

AposCon	*Apostolic Constitutions*
Apuleius: *deDeoSoc*	*On the god of Socrates*
—: *deDogmaPlat*	*On Platonic Doctrine*
—: *Meta*	*The Metamorphosis*
—: *Apol*	*Apology*
Arian: *Anab*	*Anabasis*
Aristotle: *NicEth*	*Nicomachean Ethics*
Athenaeus: *Deip*	*Learned Banquet/Deipnosophists*
Augustine: *Serm*	*Sermons*
—: *CivDei*	*City of God*
Cicero: *DeDiv*	*De Divinatione*
—: *DeRep*	*The Republic/De republica*
—: *Atticum*	*Letters to Atticus*
—: *ImpPomp*	*Speech for Pompey*
—: *InVat*	*About Vatinius*
—: *ProCluentio*	*In defense of Cluentius*
CII	Frey Corpus Inscriptionum Iudaicarum
CIL	Corpus Inscriptionum Latinarum
Clement of Alexandria: *Paed*	*Teacher/Paedigogicus*
—: *Strom*	*Miscellanies/Stromateis*
—: *Protrep*	*Exhortation/Protrepticus*
—: *ExMar*	*Exhortation to Martyrdom*
Ps-Clementine: *Hom*	*Homilies*
CodTheo	Codex Theodosianus
Columella: *RR*	*On Agriculture*
Damascius: *VitIsid*	*Life of Isidore*
Diodorus: *Siculus Hist*	*History*
Diogenes of Halicarnassus: *AntiRom*	*Roman Antiquities*
Diogenes Laertius: *Lives*	*Lives of the Philosophers*
Eunapius: *VitaPhil*	*Lives of the Philosophers*
Euripides: *Alc*	*Alcestis*
Eusebius: *PE*	*Preparation for the Gospels*
Hesiod: *Theog*	*Theogony*
Hippocrates: *SD*	*Sacred Diseases*
Hippolytus: *Ref*	*Refutations*
Horace: *Sat*	*Satires*
Iamblichus: *DeMyst*	*On the Mysteries*
IG	Inscriptiones Graecae
Irenaeus: *AdHaer*	*Against Heresies*
Josephus: *BJ*	*Jewish War*
—: *Ant*	*Antiquities*
John Chysostom: *Jud*	*Against Judaizers*
—: *Hom*	*Homilies*

—: *inPs*	*Commentary on Psalms*
Justin: *Trypho*	*Dialogue with Trypho*
—: *1Apol*	*First Apology*
—: *2Apol*	*Second Apology*
—: *Orat*	*Oration*
Lactanius: *DivInst*	*Divine Institutions*
Lucan: *BelCiv*	*CivilWar*
Lucian: *Pseudoph*	*Lover of Lies*
—: *Scyth*	*Scythians*
—: *DeorConc*	*Congregation of the Gods*
Marcus Aurelius: *Med*	*Meditations*
Marinus: *VitaPro*	*Life of Proclus*
Mig	*On the Migration of Abraham*
NHC	*Nag Hammadi Corpus*
Origen: *CC*	*Contra Celsum*
—: *ComJn*	*Commentary on John*
—: *DePr*	*First Principles*
—: *ExMar*	*Exhortation to Martyrdom*
—: *ComMatt*	*Commentary on Matthew*
Ovid: *MedFac*	*Cosmetics*
—: *ArsAmat*	*The Art of Love*
—: *RemAm*	*Remedies of Love*
PGM	*Papyri Graecae Magicae (Greek Magical Papyri)*
Philo: *Vita*	*Life of Moses*
—: *QuesEx*	*Questions on Exodus*
—: *SacAbel*	*Sacrifice of Abel*
—: *VitCon*	*On the Contemplative Life*
—: *LegAll*	*Allegorical Interpretation*
—: *De spec Leg*	*On the Special Laws*
—: *Quod omnis probus*	*Every Good Man*
—: *de Decal*	*On the Decalouge*
Pindar: *Olym*	*Olympian Odes*
Plato: *Crat*	*Cratylus*
Pliny: *NH*	*Natural History*
Plotinus: *Enn*	*Enneads*
Plutarch: *QuesCon*	*Table Talk*
—: *RomanQues*	*Roman Questions*
—: *DeDefectu*	*On the Obsolescence of Oracles*
—: *Cor*	*Coriolanus*
—: *OrDelphi*	*On the Delphic Oracles*
Porphyry: *deAbst*	*On Abstinence*
Proclus: *InTim*	*Commentary on the Timeaus*
—: *ThPl*	*Platonic Theology*
—: *InPlatRemp*	*Commentary on Republic*
—: *InCratyl*	*Commentary on Cratylus*
SHR	*Sepher Ha-Razim: The Book of Mysteries*

Seneca: *HerOet*	*Hercules Oetaeus*
Sophocles: *Antig*	*Antigone*
Statius: *Theb*	*Thebais*
Strabo: *Geo*	*Geography*
Suetonius: *Vesp*	*Vespasian*
Tacitus: *Hist*	*Histories*
Tatian: *Disc*	*Discourse Against The Greeks*
Tertullian: *deAnima*	*On the Soul*
—: *DeSpec*	*On the Shows*
—: *CultFem*	*The Cult of Women*
—: *DeBapt*	*On Baptism*
Virgil: *Ecl*	*Eclogues*

Additional Abbreviations

Ber	Berthelot and Ruelle 1963
DK	Diels and Kranz 1956
PG	Patrologia graeca

INTRODUCTION

This book is about the human imagination, and especially about hostile imagination. To call someone a "magician" during the first three centuries CE was to mount a negative and potentially damaging attack. In Christian, Jewish and Greco-Roman sources the terms we translate as "magic" and "magicians" were associated with human sacrifices, perverse sexual practices and all sorts of antisocial and misanthropic activities.

During the reign of Augustus, at the beginning of the time period of our study, the poet Horace painted a particularly gruesome picture of witches who perform not just human but child sacrifice (*Epodes* 5).[1] The craven witches bury a young boy in the sand up to his neck and tempt him with food until they finally cut out his organs for use in a love potion. At the end of the fourth century, just past the other limit for our study, Priscillian, bishop of Avila in Spain, was charged with being a heretic and a magician. The bishops who opposed him were able to have him executed, demonstrating just how lethal these charges could be.

On closer inspection these charges, and the many made in the intervening years, do not stand up to investigation. Despite Horace's vivid imagination, we have no evidence that bands of hags tortured and then killed children. Priscillian was charged with having nighttime meetings with women, praying naked and practicing sorcery. All of these charges resulted from internal disputes about church authority and conflicts among bishops about theology.[2] Jews, as we will see, were often charged with being magicians in the ancient world not because they really were such. The charges were based on stereotypes over which Jews had no control and not, of course, on some true connection Jews had with evil powers.

Charges of magic reveal social tensions, internecine battles, competition for power, and fear that other people have special powers.

Charges of witchcraft represented socially-acceptable modes of attack against political enemies when other modes of asserting rivalry were not an option. In the fourth century, for example, given the political loyalty of those around the Emperor, "resentment and anomalous power on the edge of the court could be isolated only by the now intimate allegation – sorcery" (Brown 1972: 125). In these attacks we see people trying, at best, to produce exciting literature, or at worst, to eliminate enemies and opponents. We must not confuse these attacks with sober presentations of fact; simply put, when someone calls someone else a magician, we should not take the charge at face value.

We can also track the flip-side of these attacks, that is, the less frequent cases where terms derived from the same root as "magic" are associated with much more positive, but equally imaginative, powers and knowledge. The "magi" were specialists in the very best foreign wisdom according to some ancient sources. This wisdom excelled all other since it was divine, available only from priests and the most holy philosophers.

In order to formulate a successful investigation into ancient "magic" we will have to set aside the habits and training of our own imaginations. We bring many of our own modern expectations to a study of "magic." A quick flip through the Yellow Pages reveals that "magic" in its most common use today is largely a mode of entertainment, an activity for children's parties.[3] In this social context, the skill of the magician is measured by his illusions, his ability to make a dramatic and confounding act look real even though the audience (or at least the adults who hired him) knows that every act is fake. Coming from this benign view of magic, we will be shocked to see that people are being put to death for engaging in "magic" in the first centuries CE.

Another set of modern imaginings about "magic" is to embrace the term as a means of playing with, and redirecting, the power latent in the negative social images of witchcraft. Women in particular, recognizing the oppressive use of the term "witch" in past history, claim for themselves the implicit power of the stereotype. The popular bumper sticker "My other car is a broom" hints at an alternate identity more mysterious and powerful than the normal one. Alliance with covens is made in some circles today as a countercultural move, a way of rejecting social norms.

These very modern moves are made independent of whether the individuals persecuted and killed in the past would have embraced the labels "witches" and "magician," given a choice. Many of the people labeled "magicians" in the first three centuries were simply practicing traditional forms of their religious practice. Since they were often pagans much of what people claim as "ancient magic" is modern imaginings of ancient Greco-Roman religion. The ancient practitioners would be horrified to be lumped together with "witches" and "warlocks" (though they might be happy to see the current interest in their ancient practices). They too believed that certain *other* practices were witchcraft and condemned the practitioners as magicians.

Many of these modern imaginings are far from the notions of magic in the first centuries. As we will see in Chapter 1, labeling people "magicians" was a way of marginalizing them, casting doubt on their practices and beliefs. "Magic" was not bad because it was fraudulent, though that possibility was raised at a few points in ancient discussions. In the main magic was dangerous because it *worked*. In the eyes of our ancient sources magic produced real results. It did so, however, by means of evil powers. Thus its social place was with other real and imagined practices that were thought to threaten the social fabric, such as human sacrifice and cannibalism. On a more intimate scale magic threatened one's family and prosperity.

Since the term carried with it so much opprobrium, it was rarely used as a term of self-definition.[4] Moses and Jesus were both considered magicians by outsiders, much to the horror of Jews and Christians. *Any* ritual action could be labeled "magic" from the Jewish use of phylacteries to Greco-Roman prayer ceremonies and the Christian Eucharist. Entire religions were defined as "magic," and the consequences linger today, especially in the case of modern attitudes towards Greco-Roman and Egyptian religious practices.

No doubt some ancients were skeptical of any and all attempts to employ supernatural powers, but their writings are not the focus of this study. Even the rituals such as alchemy, sometimes considered to be proto-science, attempted to transform earthly metals into divine substances.

This study will not address the limitations of modern scholarly definitions of magic, though at a few points some of the lingering influence of these definitions will be noted. The origins and shortcomings of late nineteenth to early twentieth century definitions of magic have already been discussed at length. Voluminous articles and books have been written on this topic and anyone interested in it can find many cogent discussions.[5] In briefest outline, the influential early twentieth-century formulations of "magic" such as

James Frazer's in *The Golden Bough* were based on Victorian notions of evolution. "Magic," found primarily in non-Christian religions, was an evolutionary precursor to "religion." The primitive practices were based on flawed modes of thought Frazer formulated as the Laws of Contagion and Like-Attracts-Like.[6] Evidence of these laws included an enormous mix of rituals drawn from, as they were called then, "savage" cultures. Due to his anti-Catholic attitude, Frazer also included as magic a few European peasant practices.

All these exemplary rituals were taken out of their theological and social contexts. This was key to building a synthetic picture of "magic." Since the theological explanations were missing, the practices looked nonsensical and silly. They were then contrasted to other more familiar religious practices of Protestant Christians. These latter practices either were presumed to have complex theological and philosophical foundations or were left without scrutiny as to their modes of perceived efficacy (why people thought they might work).

The shortcomings of this method of analysis have been recognized and articulated at length.[7] In addition to its misguided evolutionary assumptions, it draws deeply on the individual prejudices of the scholar and his or her imaginings about what modes of ritual action are inappropriate or simply aesthetically unappealing. Ultimately Frazer's discussion did not establish a coherent category of magical rituals distinct from religious ones, based on either the methods employed or the goals sought. The quintessential magical method, using a voodoo doll, is indistinguishable from methods used in religious rituals; at the same time, the goals of magic – improving health, destroying enemies – are now recognized as part and parcel of religious practices.

With the demise of twentieth century definitions of magic, many rituals which were classified as magic only a few decades ago have made their way back into the more acceptable category religion. A bellwether of these modifications, chosen somewhat randomly from among hundreds, is the work of Judah Goldin on Honi the Circle-Drawer. Honi appears in several rabbinic texts, each with a somewhat differing recounting of his exploits. His most famous exploit was drawing a circle on the ground and refusing to come out until the deity sent rain.[8] In Goldin's 1963 article the story of Honi the Circle-Drawer is presented as a clear example of magic, following its classification as magic by Ludwig Blau in 1914.

Influenced no doubt by the ongoing debates about definitions of magic, in a subsequent article in 1976 Goldin no longer described

Honi as a magician. Instead he noted that Honi was not declared to be a magician in any of the sources. The ancient texts refer to him as one of the "men of deed," a category of practitioners who were at odds with rabbis. From the rabbinic point of view "Honi's behavior is in fact regarded by his critics as an example of arrogance towards Heaven" (1976). The rabbis' mixed view of Honi is no doubt based in part on their competition with characters of his type.[9] Honi's ritual is not "magic" from either a rabbinic or a scholarly view, though it is clearly behavior about which the rabbis had mixed feelings.

Despite its increasingly contested status, "magic" lingers on as a substantive category in scholarly discourse. Hesitant to abandon altogether the word "magic" as a scholarly category, some scholars have called for a "common sense" definition. Others try to shore up Frazer's tottering schema and find some more systematic distinction between magic and religion. Almost across the board we find increasingly narrow definitions of magic, which one by one eliminate elements found in, for example, Blau's classic 1914 study of Jewish magic. The few items remaining in the category "magic" include an odd collection of the recitation of nonsense syllables, certain verbal formulas (commands), some negative behaviors such as cursing and the use of material objects in rites. Several of these are encountered in the texts discussed in Chapter 3; modern definitions of magic will briefly be commented on there. Sometimes what passes for analysis of Jewish magic is simply the modern repetition of ancient rabbinic prejudices against practices that they could not control.

The label "magic," in short, was too closely intertwined with polemics in the ancient world to easily, or even with a great deal of contortion, fall into a neat scholarly category.[10] The emerging consensus that defining magic is as problematic as defining vulgarity or deviance (Garrett 1989) forces us to rethink what should be covered in a book about "magic." One avenue would be to limit our analysis to cases where the rituals are not labeled as magic by someone else, but where the term appears to be a mode of self-classification. If we limit this book to rituals which were labeled as "magic" by the practitioners who enacted them, we would have a very short book. Any investigation of imagination is not an easy task and the ancient rhetorical uses of the term do not define an obvious subject matter for a book on "magic."

Our first task then, covered in Chapter 1, is to look more closely at the usages of the term "magic" in the first three centuries. The Greek term *mageia* comes from the term for a Persian priest (*magos*).

The term received a mostly negative valence due to the ambivalent, but generally hostile, attitude of Greco-Roman writers to their famous neighbors. As a placeholder for hostile imaginings, the term "magician" was juxtaposed from the fifth century BCE on with a range of suspicious practices such as divination and healing. Employed in the legal codes as a charge warranting capital punishment, *mageia* solidified into a term of abuse. Use by Jews, Christians and Greco-Roman writers was highly rhetorical, and pointed to the complex social textures of inter- and intra-group hostilities.

After the survey of ancient usages in Chapter 1, we will consider a variety of ritual practices from first three centuries CE. Each of our examples draws on data from Jewish, Christian and Greco-Roman religions. Each illustrates some aspect of the late antique artifice of employing supernatural powers. Each case will give us some insight into the construction of rituals, viewed as sanctioned by some and as illicit magic by others.

As we do so, we will move from the realm of hostile imaginings to the reverse of such attacks: how the practitioners themselves imagined their rituals to work. Here we will see individuals putting to work a variety of notions about effective words and deeds.

Given the problems with dating ritual texts, we will occasionally look at material preserved in texts that date from later centuries. This is especially true in the case of Jewish texts, where we will frequently turn to rabbinic texts edited much past the first three centuries. In these cases parallel texts from other religious traditions which are easier to date supply important evidence that the later rabbinic texts preserved ideas from earlier centuries.

The first example, discussed in Chapter 2, is exorcism, and in particular, exorcism as a method of healing. These dramatic contests lead us to the issue of daimons, the supernatural forces that could inhabit a human body. Even a brief review of the role of daimons and their place within the ancient cosmology disabuses us of modern stereotypes of monotheism. Central to the construction of these rituals is a rich, and inherently obscure, imagining of diverse types of supernatural forces. The chapter then turns to some specific examples of how human practitioners attempted to gain control over the daimons. Human suffering in the form of illness was a palpable monument to the belief that daimons could move into human homes. Curing the afflicted person was a supernatural battle that momentarily revealed the workings of a usually unseen world.

Chapter 3 turns to love-rites and the Greek and Hebrew handbooks in which they appear. Both handbooks present their rituals as a particular type of activity, one which includes the recitation of complicated verbal formulas and the use of numerous types of material objects. The handbooks include a wide variety of goals, some of which are mundane, if not downright silly. Why bother to employ supernatural power to, for example, fill up a room with smoke and thereby impress people, as found in the Hebrew *Book of Secrets*? If some rituals look suspicious due to their evil intentions, others look beneath the dignity of religious concerns. Yet the ancient texts belie these divisions and include all of these concerns together. Here again we need to consider how this wide range of rituals was thought to work. Central to this chapter is the use of material objects and their role in the perceived efficacy of the rituals.

The next chapter, Chapter 4, turns to alchemy or the "Sacred Art," as it was called in the first centuries. Early alchemical traditions present a complex case of classification for both ancients and moderns. The goals of these rites look extremely suspicious both to those who do not believe this type of transformation is possible and to those who do not want people to have such power. At the same time, the philosophical underpinnings of some of the rites, and the technical appearance of the rituals, have led many to classify the rites as somehow closer instead to science. This chapter will try to give an idea of how the ancient practitioners thought their rituals worked and how notions of natural forces in turn helped shape the contours of definitions of magic.

The next set of rituals in Chapter 5 attempts to turn humans into divine beings by conferring immortality on them. The striking, even seemingly heretical, nature of these rituals calls our attention to them. The classic picture of magic centers on the powerful figure of the magician. Rituals that turn humans into divine figures might be the best place to locate "magicians." However, these rituals place the transformed individual not outside of the bound of religious expression but as the prime representative of the highest religious strivings. What is most striking, perhaps, is the incredible range of rituals which were understood to have this goal and potential. The rites have a distinct aesthetic sense which challenges both the modern division between magic and religion and modern notions of monotheism.

The final chapter, Chapter 6, focuses directly on the issue of gender. Historically, men have done much of the imagining of magic, thus many of the people accused of perverse practices have been women. We will look at this general question from the late antique perspective and see how and why women were associated so closely with "magic." Our test case is rabbinic discussions of female witches, chosen because they offer us both extensive and highly theoretical presentations of the issues.

The intriguing question of why people believe these ideas and rituals will not be addressed in this study, but two preliminary points on this topic deserve attention. First, in order to begin thinking about why people might believe in notions of cause and effect different from ours we must start with a careful examination of the specific historical context. It is the premise of this study, learned from recent anthropological theories, that notions of cause and effect are culturally based. This is not a claim of radical relativism; some of the basic principals of logic may turn out to be cross-culturally true. Most of the time, however, people are not using strictly logical modes of thought. This leaves us plenty of room for cultural and historical variation in modes of thought about cause and effect.[11]

Second, at quite a different level, partial answers to this question may come from the world of psychology and thus are beyond the scope of this study. It is possible to induce incorrect notions of cause and effect in most people in just a few minutes. All that is necessary is to expose them to rewards which they believe they are generating based on their actions when in fact the rewards are randomly awarded.[12] People will latch onto any seeming success and repeat it, even when they have to explain repeated failures as well. It appears practically impossible, or at least very rare, for humans not to be influenced by immediate experiences of concrete results. This is true even if these experiences turn out to have limited theoretical validity. The moment of surprise is not when people repeat alchemical failures but when they begin to do something else.

Despite our desire to see ourselves as direct heirs of late antique beliefs, we must develop a sense of being visitors to this world. And most of all we must be willing to look at rituals which might seem familiar with new eyes lest we too easily join the polemical wars of the ancient world. While we begin looking at "magic" what may change for us is our notion of the contours of the human imagination.

1
GRECO-ROMAN, CHRISTIAN AND JEWISH CONCEPTS OF "MAGIC"

The origin of our term "magic" is filled with irony and imagination. The Greek term *mageia* [Latin: *magia*] derives from the Persian term *magos*: "priest."[1] This hereditary priesthood from what is now Western Iran officiated at the ancient fire sacrifices. Herodotus, whose vision was adopted by so many later Greeks, painted a vivid picture for the Greeks of the foreign priests chanting stories of the birth of the gods at the sacrifices (*Hist*. 1.132, cf. 7.43).

By the first centuries of the Common Era the term *mageia* already had a long history of use in Greek literature. The earliest Greek writer to describe the priests appears to be Xanthus in the early fifth century (Diogenes Laertes, *Lives* 1.2). He wrote an entire treatise about the foreign priests, thereby making some doctrines of ancient Persian religion available to the Greek audience.[2]

Greek uses of the term after Xanthus had negative, or at best mixed, connotations.[3] Religious terms often accrue negative connotations in another culture, as in the cases of *voodoo* or *fakir*.[4] Persians were not only foreigners but also military enemies. Magi accompanied Xerxes in his famed crossing of the Hellespont (Kingsley 1995: 189). In Greco-Roman usage the picture of the *magos* and his *mageia* deviated from the original meaning, until, as we will see, it became an umbrella term for any and all suspect uses of supernatural powers.

A variety of Greek literary texts associated the *magos* and his work of *mageia* with all sorts of questionable figures including beggars and wizards.[5] Inexplicable behavior, such as Helen leaving her husband for the Trojan Paris, was attributed to the mysterious power of these individuals (Euripides, *Orestes* 1497). The rhetorician Gorgias equated the practices of the *magoi* with *goetia*, an older Greek term for illicit and malevolent practices with even worse connotations (DK 82 B 11 p. 291).[6]

Even as *mageia* came generally to denote suspicious and barbaric practices, it continued to be used in more charitable ways in some circles.[7] The term still had positive connotations, harkening back to the *magi* and *mageia* as special and powerful esoteric practitioners and practices which were foreign but not illicit or wrong. According to the pseudo-Platonic dialogue *Alcibiades* the magi were in charge of the "worship of the gods" (1.122A). Cicero introduced the term to his first century BCE Latin readers as "augurs and diviners among the Persians," roles familiar to Roman readers (*deDiv* 1.41.90–1). In the first century CE Dio Chrysostom referred to the magi as those who specialize in the worship of the divine (*Oration* 36.4).

In the mid-second century CE, the writer Apuleius, charged by hostile relatives with luring his rich wife via magic, was able as part of a biting and often sarcastic defense to point to the positive meanings of *magos*. In his *Apology*, delivered in North Africa in 158/9 he stated,

> For if, as I read in many authors, a magician means in the language of the Persians, the same thing that the word "priest" does, I put, what is the crime, pray, in being a magician? What is the crime in properly knowing, and understanding, and being versed in the laws of ceremonials, the solemn order of sacred rites, and religious ordinances?
>
> (*Apology* 25.26)

Much later the neo-platonic philosopher Proclus (b. 410) called upon the practices of the magi as support for his positive attitude toward prayer (*inTim* 1. p. 208). Clearly he thought that his readers would recognize his reference to the ancient priests. In Jewish circles, positive descriptions of the magi include Philo's description of their attempts to learn the truth (*Quod omnis probus* 74).[8]

These were minority positions, however, and the negative usages were much more common. Thus Augustine had to explain the suspicious appearance of "magi" in the New Testament; he commented that they were common magicians who had been converted by grace (*Sermons* 20.3–4).[9]

Use of the term in Roman legal rulings was decidedly negative.[10] These usages are first documented, as best as we can tell, with the *Sententiae* of the jurist Iulius Paulus.[11] The history of this commentary to earlier law codes is obscure, but it was probably edited in the early third century CE using older materials.

In the hands of the Roman lawmakers the previous negative associations of the term were solidified. The practice of *mageia* became a capital offense.[12] Thus the code states "that it be decided that persons who are addicted to the art of magic shall suffer extreme punishment. Magicians themselves shall be burned alive" (*Sent* V. 23.17).[13]

Exactly which acts were proscribed varied from code to code and from emperor to emperor, depending most probably on which acts were thought to be most threatening at a particular point in time.[14] Caracalla, and later Constantius II, had very broad conceptions which included, for example, the use of amulets to ward off disease. Under Constantine the Great, the venerable institution of reading auguries for the purpose of divination came under attack. Any diviner who was charged with operating in a private house, instead of as part of the standard public rites, was liable to be burned alive.[15]

Given the social role of law codes, the use of the term in these codes seems to construct an objective definition of what magic *really* is. It is a mistake, however, to take these Roman uses and go back (or forward) in history looking for "magic." Prior to this time, suspect practices were proscribed on a case-by-case basis that did not necessarily reflect the later Roman notions of magic. For example, the Twelve Tables, originally composed in the mid-fifth century BCE, ordered punishment for the person "who sang evil songs" *malum carmen incantare*, and who tried to steal harvests via incantations.[16] The Latin phrasing for both injunctions is ambiguous. Ancient interpreters understood the "evil songs" to be a form of slander; modern interpreters are more likely to label it ancient "magic."[17] These injunctions were not made in reference to any abstract notion of magic, at least as far as the citations we have from the Twelve Tables. Their inclusion was based on the fact that the practices led to personal injury.

Plato also argued for punishing instances of harm done against individuals without any reference to an overarching category of "magic."[18] Plato's discussion is particularly subtle and it distorts his complex classification to simply say that Plato was legislating against "magic." When someone was harmed, the first question that had to be asked, according to Plato, was the social role of the person who harmed him (*Laws* 933C–E). A doctor could be punished for harming an individual while the actions of a private person carried fewer social consequences. Again this usage is distinct from later Roman ones.

In the first century BCE Sulla's *Lex Cornelia de Sicariis et Veneficis* constructed a special class of outlawed political plotters and poisoners. *Veneficium* were potions that were thought, among other things, to heal or to cause people to fall in love. Sometimes they were lethal.[19] Again the ruling is specific and no general category is referred to. In fact, references to *veneficium* throughout Roman literature, and to Φάρμακον in Greek literature, are always ambiguous.[20] The potions were powerful; whether that power was for good or for evil depended on the outcome of each specific case.[21]

The appearance of the term "magic" in law codes gives us a series of snapshots of abstract social usage, but does not begin to demarcate the social employment of the term in attacks and counterattacks. Who was charged with these offences, and who was, beyond that, convicted and punished, depends on issues at which the code does not even hint. In addition, the fact that any event (or non-event) could be explained as due to magic meant that tremendous weight was always thrown on rhetorical arguments even when used in legal settings.

We see this in Apuleius' lively defense against the legal charge that he was a magos and that he had seduced his wife via magic.[22] Despite attempts in the law codes to delineate a clear set of forbidden activities, the specific components in the charge of magic made against him included actions as diverse as collecting fish, owning a mirror, writing poetry, and having a suspiciously small number of servants. "Magic" refused to stay within a neat set of legal definitions.

Apuleius readily pointed out that no one action with which he was charged inherently constitutes magic: is everyone who collects fish a magician? Many of the activities which look like magic, he argued, are in fact the daily pursuits of philosophers and those who investigate the natural world. Seen from this angle, the practices appear innocent, or even praiseworthy. Equally important to Apuleius was a general strategy of ridiculing his opponents. He attempted to put them on the defensive by casting doubt on their characters and motives and thereby to impugn the entire case.

Not everyone was equally likely to be charged as a magician. In addition to the magi, several other groups were particularly closely associated with magic. Hebrews and Jews were thought to have access to ancient secrets, sometimes understood to be helpful wisdom and sometimes viewed more negatively as forbidden and perverse magical practices.[23] Egypt was often cited as the source of magic by other cultures. A writing system which pre-dated the

Greeks and the enormous ancient monuments impressed Herodotus and thereby all Greeks. Hieroglyphs, mummification, elaborate priesthoods – all these made Egypt a convenient source for strange and perverse knowledge. Already in the text of Isaiah, Egypt was posited as the source of necromancy rituals by the deuteronomic redactor (Schmidt 1994: 188). This trope reappears in rabbinic literature in the saying that nine tenths of magic was given to Egypt (*Avot R Nat* 48). For Origen the main contemporary practitioners of magic were located in Egypt (*CC* 1.22, 28, 38, 68).

Thrace was considered to be the home of many magicians, as was Thessaly, which was notorious for its witches.[24] The Marsi were known as "snake-charmers" with special cures for snakebites, a cliché from Ovid (*MedFac* 39) to Augustine (*Epist* 55.12; *Gen ad litt* 21.28, 29). All of these stereotypes flourished in the first three centuries CE and some continue to thrive today.

Pliny's critique of the magi

In the second half of the first century CE, Pliny composed his magisterial *Natural History*, a compendium of information about the natural world. This extended survey compiles a hodgepodge of information about plant and animal products including their uses in curing diseases. Pliny tantalizes us by offering to "expose" the "fraudulent lies of the magi" whose "art has held complete sway throughout the world for many ages" (*NH* 30.1). Modern readers, eager to prove that educated Romans rejected "magic," have often pointed to Pliny's rejection of the magi. His compendium, they argue, approaches the world through careful empirical observation rather than through magic. Pliny's dismissal of magical cures looks deceptively modern at first glance and appears to set him up as a reasoned critic of magical practices.

Pliny, however, includes cures modern readers would never dream of employing. His conception of magic is inconsistent and highly rhetorical, permitting him to both include and exclude practices at will. On closer analysis we see that he does not use a coherent set of criteria for evaluating the ideas of the magi, or anyone else's cures for that matter. His definition of magic cannot be ours.

The magi's success is due, Pliny warned, to their ability to make a combination of medicine, religion and astrology that is irresistible to most people (*NH* 30.2). Many famous thinkers were drawn to this philosophy and treasured the magi's secrets, including Pythagoras, Empedocles, Democritus and even Plato (*NH* 30.9). Pliny was bewildered that Homer did not refer to the magi and their arts, since characters in Homer's poems practice arts which look to him like those of the magi (*NH* 30.5–6).

When it comes to explaining in more detail the particular reasons for rejecting the cures of the magi, Pliny's overall criteria are never clearly stated. Sometimes the denunciations are very specific. For example, he denounced cures of the magi for relying on "that very loathsome animal the tick (*NH* 30.82)" and on moles, animals which he thinks are "cursed by nature." Yet he can also state with confidence "I find that a heavy cold clears up if the sufferer kisses a mule's muzzle (*NH* 30.31)."

Elsewhere Pliny castigated the magi for collecting nail parings and putting them on people's doorposts, yet putting the same parings in amulets he deemed useful (*NH* 28.86). The reason why he rejected putting them on people's doorposts is that he worries that this practice might spread a disease. The mechanism for this contagion is unclear. The critique appears to be ad hoc: fear of spreading disease, for whatever reason, does not re-appear often in his writings.

The only consistent criterion that Pliny used is that he rejected the notion, which he attributed to the magi, of collecting medicinal materials based on the phases of the moon and other astrological considerations (*NH* 28.95). He held to this position consistently, rejecting cures with astrological components even when they are not associated with the magi (*NH* 30.96). The idea of correlating earthly cures found in nature with the movement of the moon and stars appears to be too complicated for Pliny. He did not completely discount these cures, rejecting only the method of gathering the materials. He accepted, for example, the view of the magi about the power of hyena skin, but rejected their claim that the hyenas must be hunted during a particular phase of the moon (*NH* 28.94).

Pliny also rejected cures which seemed overly elaborate to him. In one revealing instance he criticized a cure simply because it required fifty-four different ingredients. The sheer complexity of the recipes seemed to make it suspicious (*NH* 29.24–5).

The denunciations of the magi, rather than being a clear critique of "magic," were part of Pliny's strategy to bolster the reputation of his own research. Pliny tried to set apart some cures as more reliable than others. He reinforced the quality of approved cures by dotting his work with references to authorities who successfully cured specific people by the procedures he compiled. Midway in his report about cures that employ bird organs he recounted that the Aspenates brothers, from a consular family, were cured of colic. He was able not only to name the individuals, but also give the specifics of the cures: one brother wore an amulet made from a lark and the other offered up a bird-derived sacrifice at a brick oven (*NH* 30.20).

These very specific authorities and cures contrast with references to fraudulent authorities such as the "magi" and "doctors." The latter he denounced with fervor and quite a lot of wit (*NH* 29.1–28). Doctors, for example, are "the only people who can commit homicide with impunity" (*NH* 29.18). Their practices are based on whim as they "change their minds a thousand times" (*NH* 19.23). Their main concern is to collect huge fees for themselves.

Pliny did not, however, reject all cures used by doctors. His model was Cato, who denounced doctors, all the while keeping his own book of cures which he employed for the benefit of his family and slaves (*NH* 29.14–16).

Since Pliny had few other means of establishing the reasonability of his mode of work, lacking anything like clinical trials or testing of specific ingredients, he had to set up the straw men of greedy doctors and astrological magi. The impressive specificity of Pliny's knowledge about good cures is contrasted with specific failures of the magi and the doctors. Pliny could point to a Roman nobleman who wore a special egg recommended by the magi and was killed by the emperor precisely because it was discovered (*NH* 29.52–4).

Pliny stressed that he did not undertake his compendium for personal gain (unlike the doctors) and that he had judiciously weeded out, or signaled to the reader, the more outlandish cures (unlike the magi). These rhetorical claims do not make Pliny's collection a forerunner of modern empirical science and medicine. Rejecting the collection of materials based on the phases of the moon as well as concoctions which have more than fifty-four ingredients does not make his guidebook rational.

In the end Pliny's theory of efficacy for the cures he favored was the same one employed by other people in cures he rejected: the concepts of *discordia* [antipathy] and *concordia* [sympathy]. These terms were widely used in the first three centuries CE to refer to a general belief in multiple interconnections between disparate parts of the natural world.[25] Pliny offered examples such as "the magnetic stone draws iron to itself while another kind repels it, the diamond, unbreakable by any other force is broken by goat's blood" (*NH* 20.2). Sympathy and antipathy are natural forces to him. From these ideas, Pliny states, "medicine" was born (*NH* 24.4).

When we look at the specifics of his cures it is often hard to see these principles systematically applied. Any one item, such as the bark of a tree, or an organ from an animal, could be used for a bewildering variety of physical complaints. For anyone who does not accept the existence of such forces, as in the case of much modern analysis, they are characterized as magic.[26]

Pliny did not even hint at a distinction between magical and religious cures; this distinction carries no valence for him. Here Pliny is similar to the early Greek medical writers, who also sweep the magi into a larger category of fraudulent practitioners, all of whom they oppose. Hippocrates, for example, in his *On the Sacred Disease*, denounced the magi together with "purifiers, charlatans and humbugs" (*SD* 2). None of these figures had any good explanations for disease.

Hippocrates distinguished these practitioners from those who bring "prayers and sacrifices." This general reference offers a simplified and idealized contrast for the "humbugs." It makes no attempt to explain what the role of the prayers and sacrifices are in relation to the cures advocated by the Hippocratic writers. Some of the figures denounced would probably be described in modern terms as "religious" practitioners. All of these figures, according to Hippocrates, do not understand the origin of illness and thus their attempts to cure people are destined to fail.[27]

Pliny had no need of a more refined (or more consistent) definition. His magi no longer officiated at fire sacrifices, but instead are connected with a welter of healing practices. Constructing a path between the doctor and the magi, Pliny sought a course that looked reasonable and judicious. Western attacks on Chinese medicine might offer us a modern parallel. These practices often lack the institutional basis other forms of medicine have in the West and represent a threatening foreign wisdom. This analogy reminds us that there is nothing inherently "magical" about the healing practices of the magi, and we have no idea if they were any more or less successful than those Pliny advocated.

The church fathers' views of magic

In religious debates during the first three centuries charges of magic were used in numerous ways to draw distinctions between insiders and outsiders, and between proper and improper practices and beliefs. At the simplest level "magic" was the term used for other people's religious rituals (Neusner 1989). Christian and Greco-

Roman writers denounced as magic Jewish practices of fasting, food restrictions and Sabbath observance.[28] Jews in turn denounced Jesus as a magician, though the subsequent censorship of rabbinic texts often disguised the stories so that the references to Jesus must be reconstructed.[29] Jews and Christians condemned "pagan" rituals as magic. As one example among many, for Justin his turn to Christianity was a turn away from magic (*1Apol.* 14).[30] No doubt Greco-Roman writers engaged at points in similar polemics.[31]

It would be a mistake to leave the discussion at the level of these isolated comments. Out of context, these comments loom large and are likely to lead us to see them as representations of general patterns of group interactions. Not every equation of a practice with "magic" was equally vicious and many were no doubt used for internal consumption among, for example, Christian readers.

Just as important for our purposes, these types of individual comments tend to disguise the more nuanced edges of ancient uses of the term, as we saw in Pliny's case. These basic inter-group charges do not exhaust the rhetorical uses of the term "magic" in religious debates in the first centuries. Early Christian writers used the term "magic" differently depending on the type of text an author was writing and on his intended audience. The use was inseparable from the larger rhetorical goals.

Irenaeus, the fractious and always combative bishop of Lyon, did not waste much ink on pagans as magicians because his real battles were with other Christians. He yoked "heretic" and "magician" together in order to marginalize his Christian opponents and their followers, including Simon, Menander, Carpocrates and Basilides. He wove together every pejorative word he could find, describing Marcus as "very skilled in magical imposture" and the "forerunner of the Antichrist" (*AdHaer* 1.13.1).

The success of Irenaeus' enemies in recruiting and retaining adherents particularly irked and threatened him and was specifically attributed to magic (*AdHaer* 1.13.1–6). Their "magic," Irenaeus admits to his chagrin, appears to work. His enemies flourish and their circles of influence grow. Here Irenaeus sounded a note very similar to that of the author of Acts, who attributed the success of Simon, a competing Christian proselytizer, to magic. Simon was able to gain followers, according to the author of Acts, only because he used sorcery and bewitched them (Acts 8:9).

For Irenaeus the charge of magic conveniently packaged with it an explanatory tool: his enemies flourish due to the help of daimons.[32] That is, Irenaeus' enemies have effective supernatural powers on their side who bring about their successes. But these powers are evil. In the case of major opponents, Satan himself may be behind their successes (*AdHaer* 1.15.6). Their success in and of itself is no guarantee that their work is the work of God.

Irenaeus also raised the possibility that some of his opponents' successes were due not only to daimonic power but also to outright fraud. Thus they are guilty of both "magical deceptions and universal deceit" (*AdHaer* 1.4.7). The theme of magic as a form of fraud surfaced in many ancient discussions of magic. It functioned as one more aspersion to cast at opponents, appearing alongside, and not seeming to effect, a general belief that *mageia* is the effective use of supernatural forces. Thus Irenaeus was suspicious about the efficacy of some practices but basically accepted the idea that other people could manipulate evil powers and thereby do magic (*AdHaer* 2.32.5).

For Irenaeus the charges remained at the level of name-calling, unlike the later case of Priscillian who was executed by his enemies as a heretic and magician. Irenaeus did not have the political means to punish other Christians as magicians. Irenaeus' theory does not appear to be uniquely Christian. He considers the possibility that some actions called magic may simply be fraudulent, while his real concern was with effective actions powered by evil forces. All of these ideas he shared with non-Christian neighbors.

For those Christian writers who were not bishops, and therefore were less involved in issues of authority, terms associated with *mageia* were employed in completely different rhetorical flourishes. Clement of Alexandria, for example, spiced up his prose with imagery of charms, spells, and incantations in his writings. The deity is the "holy charmer of sick souls" (*Paed* 1.2) and his love is directed to people via a "love-charm" (*Paed* 1.3). Nor was Clement suspicious of the magi. He claimed a relationship with previous Greek philosophers who in turn had studied with assorted foreign wise men among whom were the magi. They taught, among others, Pythagoras (*Strom* 1.15).

Apologetic Christian texts, which defended Christians and Christianity against charges of magic, perforce offered extensive defenses of Christian practice. Simply to declare "you do magic, and I don't" was inadequate since the practices being defended were often indistinguishable from forbidden ones. It was necessary to set forth in some detail the basis for the classification of an action as either *mageia* or not.

Origen outlined his beliefs about magic in his treatise *Contra Celsum*, his attempt to refute the Greco-Roman writer Celsus' anti-

Christian attacks.[33] Origen's comments in this treatise, and other remarks scattered in his extensive corpus, outline his lines of defense and lead us through highly-nuanced strategies for classifying rituals as magic. At the simplest level, Origen repeated Irenaeus' point that some magic is deemed mere trickery, such as making a mirage banquet appear or vivifying non-living beings (*CC* 1.68). Here Origen found himself agreeing with a Jew mentioned by his opponent Celsus, who also cast a skeptical eye on some seemingly supernatural events: perhaps they were juggling tricks (*CC* 2.55; 3.33).

More serious than these tricks were real acts of magic, that is, actions which in the eyes of the observer put some form of supernatural power into play. One of the main explanations for these events, as we have already seen, was that they were the work of daimons.[34] Thus Origen is quick to condemn all Greco-Roman religion as magic dependent on evil daimonic forces (*CC* 5.5; 7.69; 8.2).[35] Pointing to daimons explains why their rites are both successful and wrong; pagans do, for example, know how to use songs to heal people.[36] The efficacy of these acts does not legitimate these actions since they are based on the work of evil forces.

Explanations based on daimons had their limits, however. By general agreement daimons have a limited sphere of influence. Healing and predicting the future were daimonic specialties, according to both Celsus and Origen (*CC* 8.58). Daimons may, for example, heal by trickery, taking over a body and then leaving it so that it appears as if they have healed the person (Tatian, *Disc,* Chap 18.3). More sophisticated occurrences are less likely to be their handiwork.

More complex criteria were needed for analyzing Jewish and, of course, Christian rituals. Origen left the status of Old Testament miracles on an ambiguous footing and is even more ambivalent on the question of whether Christians engage in magic. Heretical Christians might do magic, he admits, but there are not too many of them left (*CC.* 1.57). Rituals done by good Christians could not be magic, *by definition*, for Origen.[37]

Most revealing is Origen's schema of multiple interpretations for the same event, a schema that shows the delicate hand with which interpretation must be carried out. Origen stressed that a specialist must sift through rumors to uncover the truth. Some testimony about an event is simply lies (πλάσματα), some witnesses are deceived by daimons (*CC* 3.31), and others are simply misled by their own guilty consciences (*CC* 3.36).

Given the fact that Christian rituals were uncomfortably close to suspect practices, the best that Origen could do was to muddy the waters. All the human foibles and uncertainties he mention make classification elusive. It is hard to know exactly what magic is after reading Origen's discussion, and that, in itself, may be his best defense.

Rabbinic classification of magic

Rabbinic discussions of magic are very subtle and elaborate; they were edited over a period of centuries (third to seventh) and both benefited from and synthesized much prior debate. In general, the anecdotes about magic in rabbinic literature repeat themes familiar from Origen, though often in more technical presentations. The fulcrum of their presentations is the astounding leeway in the limits and definitions of magic. Rabbinic sources do not automatically classify anything as "magic." When identifying an act as magic, a series of questions must be asked to arrive at a correct classification. The criteria are multifaceted and subjective. The content of these questions will be familiar from Origen and Greco-Roman discussions, but the form will be true to rabbinic modes of argumentation.

In rabbinic literature strategies of definition are often as important as the definitions themselves. Learning to declare the unclean clean, presented as a criterion for serving as a judge, is a case in point. A rabbi can forbid an action as magic in one case yet in another case permit a similar action. Based on this strategy it is impossible to construct a simple list of the components of magic. Hence the frustration modern scholars encounter when they try to pinpoint exactly what constitutes "magic" for the rabbis.[38] Such discussions involve a great deal of back-pedaling; after claiming that rabbis forbid any forms of "magic," it is then necessary to explain why they engaged in or permitted so many practices which look suspiciously like magic. It is tempting, but wrong, to repeat the rabbinic prejudice that rabbis condescended to these actions based on pressure from ignorant (i.e. non-rabbinic) Jews.

An obvious place to look for precursors to the rabbinic ideas is Biblical notions of magic. This comparison is complicated by the lack of critical analysis of Biblical theories of magic. Most scholarship on magic in the Hebrew Scriptures fails to note the polemical dimensions of the texts.[39] The equation of non-Israelite religion, or alternative versions of Israelite religion, with magic, is repeated as if it is a simple description and not a rhetorical stance.

Every Biblical text which mentions a term glossed as "magic" or "magician" in modern discourse does so to make a highly polemical point.[40] Sometimes the "magicians" are the wise men and prophets of other cultures, as in the case of the Egyptian wise men in conflict with Moses. Sometimes the practitioners and prophets who were denounced operated outside of the approved realm of the Biblical editors. Deuteronomy 18:11, for example, forbids a number of types of practitioners such as the שאל אוב: "he who inquires of the One-who-Returns" and ידעני: "the Knower".[41] Other practitioners, imprecisely translated, include מכשף: "augurer," (Deut 18:10, Ex 7:11, Isa 47:9,12), הבר הבר: "charmer" (Deut 18:11, Ps 58:6), מעונן: "soothsayer" (Deut 18:10), אשף: "enchanter" (Dan 1:20 and 2:2), קסם "diviner" (Deut 18:10), and "whisperer" (Jer 8:17; Ps 58:6; Qoh 10:11; and Isa 3:3).

Many of these practices were part of Israelited religion. They did not, however, find favor with the later Deuteronomic editor. The editor therefore recast the practices as part of Canaanite religion in order to make their practice that much more scandalous.[42]

We see similar denunciations of Temple practices by the prophets. These freelance social critics objected to rituals which had been taking place in the Israelite Temple for generations. Thus Micah 3:6–7 denounces seers who operated in the Temple, but were not part of what Morton Smith called the "Yahweh-only" party (1987). These figures were generally denounced as false prophets, using the terms which had come to be associated with magic.[43]

Many of the Biblical terms for ancient practitioners were probably already obscure in the first centuries CE. The terms were reworked in rabbinic sources. Thus שאל אוב: "he who inquires of the One-who-Returns" was given the surprising interpretation of someone who raises a spirit via his male organ (bSanh 65b).[44] The ידעני: "he who inquires of the Knower" was understood to be someone who uses the bone of the Yidoa bird to give oracles (bSanh 65b). These two figures are contrasted as someone who brings up the dead person right-side up and does not violate the Sabbath while the other brings up his dead person upside-down and violates the Sabbath. These rabbinic interpretations reflect contemporary ideas of divination far-off from the ancient concepts.

Biblical and rabbinic strategies for classifying acts as magic do overlap in part. The equation of magic and idolatry (2 Kings 21:6; 2 Chron 33:6; mSanh 7:7), the suspicion that women are likely to engage in magic and the legal stance that magic is a capital offense[45] are common. Beyond these, the rabbinic criteria are similar to those found in Greco-Roman discussions of magic and not simple expansions of Biblical concepts.

At the heart of the rabbinic notion of magic is a series of questions, a classification system based on a set of criteria which can be articulated and then used to measure various cases. Was the act an illusion, or was it real? This issue is the starting point for the most extended collection of anecdotes about magic in the Talmud (bSanh 65a–67b).[46] This masterful and dense discussion synthesizes in a small space a large number of complex rulings on magic. Here the Mishnah states "The sorcerer (מכשף) who performs an act is liable for punishment, but the one who creates an illusion, is not" (mSanh 7:11). The technical term for illusion is (אחיזת עינים): "tricking the eyes." Interpretations of this ruling vary tremendously.[47] We already encountered this standard with Origen, and through him with Celsus and an un-named Jew.

Not every person who claimed to be able to engage supernatural powers actually did so. Illusions could fool an unsuspecting person who took what he saw at face value and did not realize, as a specialist would, that no material change in the cosmos had taken place. Illusions by their very nature are less likely to leave evidence.

> Rab said to Rabbi Hiyya, I myself saw an Arabian traveler take a sword and cut up a camel; then he rang a bell, at which the camel arose. He replied, "After that was there any blood or dung? But that was merely an illusion."
>
> (bSanh 67b; cf. jSanh 7:13)

Rabbah created a man but he was unable to answer Rabbi Zera's questions, proving that the supposed man was an illusion instead of a real person (bSanh 65b). Illusions may be exempt from punishment but still fall into the category of forbidden. The analogy in the text is Sabbath laws, where some actions are not punishable but are nevertheless forbidden. Illusions, in the final analysis, are a subcategory of magic, but not a very important one. Not being consumer activists, rabbis were less interested in fraud than in the real use of supernatural power.

The enigmatic ruling from the Mishnah is illustrated with a story: Rabbi Eliezer ben Hyrcanus demonstrated to Rabbi Akiba how to fill a field instantaneously with cucumbers and then to reap them (bSanh 65b). In this case the practice is permitted, since it is necessary to study certain phenomena in order to understand them. The intention of an action determines its classification.[48] This ruling is a tremendous escape clause against charges of improper practices.[49]

Was the act helpful to someone? Sanhedrin states that an act which has beneficial results is not magic (bSanh 67b). This principle was well established by Origen's time (*CC* 6.40). Jesus' actions benefited mankind, Origen argued, by reducing daimons to impotence. They could not, therefore, have been magic (*CC* 7.17; 8.43; *ComJn* 1.37). Under Constantine, attempts to help people were not criminal, nor was trying to protect a harvest from a thunderstorm.[50]

This concept leaves room for the numerous healing rituals used by rabbis.[51] The principle, however, is by no means ubiquitous or consistently applied in rabbinic stories. To give one example, reciting charms, even if the action is to prevent an animal from doing harm, is banned in the same discussion (bSanh 65a).

The analogous principle, that magic harms, appears in a fanciful etymology that the Biblical word glossed as magic, כשף, comes from the root לחש: "disrupts" (bSanh 67b). Magic "disrupts" the power of the divine family, that is, the good supernatural forces which surround the deity.[52]

Was the deed perpetrated by a suspicious person, such as a woman? This criterion is by no means unique to the rabbis but they embraced it with conspicuous enthusiasm. While men are theoretically as capable of indulging in magic as women are, the gender skewing is striking.[53] In an exegesis stunning in comparison to any remark about women and magic found in any oral culture, Exodus 22:17 is said to refer to female witches since "most women are involved in witchcraft" (bSanh 67a). Sometimes the identity of the women referred to is ambiguous,[54] but in others it is Jewish women who are being discussed. The daughters of Israel, we are told, are "addicted" to magical practices (bErub 64b). Crossroads were considered to be places where supernatural beings lurked. Hence two women sitting facing each other at a crossroads are surely engaged in magic (bPes 111a). This warning comes complete with a formula that men can use to protect themselves from the women's malevolent practices.

The flexibility of determining what is "magic" is nicely illustrated in the "Ways of the Amorites," an eclectic catalogue of suspect practices.[55] Many of these practices were common in the Greco-Roman world, including putting amulets on horses, wearing special haircuts, and inserting objects into the walls of houses (H. Lewy 1893). The import of ascribing these practices to the Amorites, biblical enemies, is somewhat obscure. A similar usage appears in Jubilees 29:11 where the Amorites are described as "wicked and sinful, and there is no people today which have equaled all of their sins." Goldin's suggestion that "Amorite" may be a metathesis for "Romai" is the most convincing explanation to date (1963: 117). The term marginalized these practices as originating in another culture and thus not being Jewish. They are not, however, all lumped together and condemned simply as "magic." The rites may have been so common that the rabbis could not convincingly classify them as magic.

The "Ways of the Amorites" are presented to the reader as a bewildering list of customs stripped of any context or explanation and forbidden. Yet, in various rulings rabbis permit practices which are identical to those in the "Ways of the Amorites." Slight contrasts distinguish between forbidden and acceptable practices (Goldin 1963). Leaving a light near a corpse in order to discomfort the dead is forbidden. Doing so in order to help the soul find its way back, is permitted.[56] Throwing an iron object into a cemetery and calling out "*Hada*" is forbidden, while throwing an iron object into a cemetery in order to nullify sorcery is permitted.[57] Tying a red string around a finger is forbidden; tying it around any other part of the body is permitted.[58] Since the only way to tell exactly which "Way of the Amorites" was permitted was to ask a rabbi, this strategy effectively brought the practices within their sphere of power.

Occasionally the mechanism for "rabbinization" is laid out for us. Suspending dates on a barren date-tree is not among the "Ways of the Amorites" because of a proof-text from Leviticus that states "And he shall cry 'Unclean, unclean.'"[59] Just as the cry of the leper may arouse pity, so too may the sight of the dates, and people will then pray for the date tree.[60] Since a theological basis for the success of the practice was elaborated, the practice became acceptable.

Reinterpretation of a "Way of the Amorites" can also be carried out by examining an act based on other rabbinic rulings. In a sweeping judgment attributed to Rabbi Johanan, a "Way of the Amorites" is permitted if it has some healing benefit (jShab 6.9, bShab 67a). Even if the ruling was not unique to the rabbis, its implementation was under rabbinic control. Once again the system of classification is the key.

It is no coincidence that the Talmud rules that anyone wishing to be on the Sanhedrin must be able to do magic (bSanh 17a). This statement locates the pragmatic act of employing power at the center of any debate. Knowing how to classify something as magic is insufficient when "magic" is understood to have real efficacy. A real expert must also know how to trump suspect use of powers. At the same time, throughout the rabbinic anecdotes debating magic is made to look as if it is simply an issue of taxonomy (to which category does this act belong?). The taxonomic debate disguises the power play behind the system.

The fantastic rhetorical success of these rabbinic presentations is seen in their longevity. Even today we wonder about the origins of the "Ways of the Amorites" and are likely to accept the classification of these actions as non-Jewish. It is easy to be caught up in rabbinic debates about whether act X or Y *really* is magic. The cryptic debates are an amazing achievement, leading us from question to question without permitting us to step back and analyze the artifice of their entire debate.

Ironically, at the same time that the rabbis were developing their criteria for why other people's rituals were magic, powerful stereotypes circulated about Jews as magicians. Greek literature barely mentions either Israelites or Hebrews prior to the time of Alexander the Great (Momigliano 1975: 74–82). When they do begin to receive notice, it is as a nation of philosophers and "priestly sages of the type the East was expected to produce" (Momigliano 1975: 86). Their "alien wisdom" was often viewed with respect,[61] but in some cases with suspicion and fear.

Not surprisingly this image lead to the charge that Jews engaged in magic.[62] The theme appears periodically in Greek and Roman texts from Posidonius' claim that Jews were sorcerers who use urine and other malodorous liquids (Strabo, *Geo* 16.2.43) to Pliny's statement that magic comes from the Jews (*NH* 30.11) and Celsus' statement that Jews are addicted to magic (*CC* 1.26).[63] As Robert Wilken writes, "What distinguished Jewish magic, at least in the minds of many people in the ancient world, was that Jewish magicians were more successful" (1983: 85).

These stereotypes also appear in Christian writings. Justin, for example, considered all Jewish rituals identical to pagan rites with their "magical fumigations and incantations" (*Trypho* 85.3). John Chrysostom told Christians that it was better to die than be healed by Jewish "charms, incantations and amulets" (*Jud* 8.5.935; 8.7. 937–8). His denunciations claimed, among other things, that daimons live in synagogues (*Hom* 1.6). The Council of Laodicea prohibited "Judaizing." This was understood as the adoption of magical practices, including the use of phylacteries (*Canon* 35–7).

One result of the centuries old equation of Jews with powerful and esoteric knowledge is that anything associated with the Jews and their history (objects, names, phrases) was included in ritual texts by people who were not Jews. The Jewish divine names, for example, were widely viewed in late antiquity as being among the most powerful ones, and therefore most likely to make a rite work. The Hebrew language, often without any idea of what the words meant, was also thought to be particularly effective.

It is a mistake, however, to ignore the distinct settings and types of texts in which these claims were made. It is not clear that the daily interactions between Jews and non-Jews, especially early on in our period of interest, were dominated by visions of magical Jews.[64] The literary stereotypes do not outweigh the extensive evidence that Jewish communities throughout the Mediterranean thrived during this period. Those instances where there was conflict centered on other issues.

With the increasing Christianization of the Roman Empire, Judaism and paganism became more consistently suspect as pejorative stereotypes gained the upper hand. Augustine repeats Seneca's denunciation of Judaism as "superstitio judaica" (*CivDei* 16.11). The origins of the term "superstition" are hotly debated; early usages connect it with divination and excessive fear of gods. In Theophrastus' famous portrait of the superstitious man we find an individual whose fear of the gods dominates his mental horizon. The term continued to be used to refer to this excessive fear; with the rise of Christianity, however, Greco-Roman rituals were labeled "superstitio." Legislation against "superstitio" could then, for example, outlaw traditional modes of divination while also taking a swipe at pagan religious beliefs in general (Salzman 1987).

The debates prefigure most of the elements of modern discourse about magic, but not in the same proportion. Fraud was a part of the equation, but more important was any use of supernatural power which was suspect in the eye of the beholder. While the specific content of the various authors' ideas of what is magic varied quite widely from author to author, we have found striking consistency in the criteria used to talk about the issue of "magic." Did an action harm someone? Who did it? What kind of effect did it have? Was it done via evil powers? People from various religious traditions shared these criteria across the board. This is the closest we can get to some notion of "late antique magic."

2
DAIMONS AND ANGELS AND THE WORLD OF EXORCISM

Staying over night in a house of study,[1] crushing a louse on one's clothing,[2] sitting under a drainpipe[3] – in the first centuries many seemingly simple activities exposed people to danger from evil spirits. At the same time other supernatural figures aided and watched over humans. In a world where all sorts of powers were at work it was hard to sort them all out.[4]

Angels, though they could bring blessings into one's life, could also be "fallen angels" who caused harm.[5] Other malevolent beings were referred to in Hebrew (and Aramaic) texts as רוחות: "spirits"[6] or מזקים: "damagers"[7] and in Greek texts as δαίμων: "daimons" (Latin: *daimon*). Augustine thought that all daimons were evil, and the term is often translated accordingly in Christian texts as "demons." This was not however, the most common usage in the first centuries. Augustine himself cited earlier Latin writers who used the word interchangeably with angels (*CivDei* 9.19). In this study, therefore, the more neutral transliteration "daimon" will be used.

The activities of angels and daimons were so "infinitely diverse" it is hard to find any situation for which they were not held responsible (Cumont 1907: 173). All types of misfortunes – sudden illness, the lost of an important item, trouble in love – were likely to be the result of daimonic activity. All types of blessings were the work of an angel.

These explanations were deemed true regardless of religious tradition. Jews, Christian and pagans all looked towards both angels and daimons as integral parts of their lives. Sometimes the obsession with these figures led opponents to claim, for example, that Jews worshipped angels (Col 2:18).[8] At the same time claims about angels were claims of closeness to the supernatural world. Celsus protested the Jews' claim that God sent angels only to them (*CC* 5.41).

Studying daimons is a challenge since daimons as such cannot be studied directly. A person getting off a plane and asking to see Hollywood is often surprised that there is no single place that constitutes Hollywood. Seeing Hollywood involves a cluster of activities such as touring the homes of stars, visiting studios, and viewing the famous sign in the Hollywood Hills. So too we never see daimons directly, but must trace the secondary evidence of their existence through the eyes of people in the first three centuries CE. They draw our attention to the evidence of the work of daimons: overturned pots, odd markings on the floors, and the wear and tear of rabbis' clothes.

The rise of angelology and daimonology

The rich multitude of supernatural figures who flourished in texts from the first three centuries CE was to some extent familiar from earlier periods. The ancient Greek world had known numerous gods, daimons, angelic messengers (Hesiod, *Theog* 781; Pindar, *Olym* 8.82), and shades of the dead. Despite modern stereotypes of ancient Israelite monotheism, Biblical texts mention the gods of other nations and a repertoire of other supernatural figures.

We find general references to large groups of angels[9] supplemented by specific references to the cherubim,[10] seraphim (Isa 6:1–2), "creatures" (Ezek 1:5), and the angel of the Lord.[11] These are contrasted, on the negative side, by threatening figures such as shedim (Deut 32:17; Ps 106:37) and se'rim (Isa 13:21; 34:14; Lev 17:7; 2 Chron 11:15). Lilith, who will become a major figure in later centuries, is mentioned once (Isa 34:14). Figures such as the sons of God (Gen 6:4; Job 1:6; 2:1; 38:7; Ps 29:1 and Wis 5:5) and the female consort of Yahweh known as Asherah remain obscure, probably repressed due to the increasingly monotheistic view of the Biblical editors.[12]

Most important for our investigation, in the Bible angels are primarily messengers who bring messages from the deity to humanity (Newsom 1992: 248). These messengers had the physical appearances of humans in both Biblical and Greek texts.[13] It was impossible to tell at first glance whether a stranger was simply a foreigner or an angel.

None of these figures were individualized with specific names and personalities until late Biblical texts such as Daniel. The divine messengers operate as nameless visitors or groups of "hosts" who praise or accompany the deity. They lack histories or personalities and do not interact with humans as part of daily life. The shocking story of the sons of God coming down to earth and having intercourse with humans results in freakish beings and is placed ominously by the Biblical editor right before the declaration of the corruption of earth (Gen 6:1–4).

Later Biblical texts were increasingly less likely to have the deity appear on earth himself; instead delegating interactions with humans to some form of representative. These supernatural representatives were described as either the deity's Name (1 Kings 8:16,29) or his angel. The use of these substitutes engendered endless theological speculation (and debate) since the manner in which they represent or stand for the deity is not always clear: Is the Name the same as the deity himself? What is the difference between the deity and his angelic presence?

By the first centuries CE religious texts presupposed a very different vision of the world than the earliest Biblical texts, including both the place of human beings and the roles of deity, angels and daimons. In short, a much more complex angelology and daimonology developed. Later Biblical texts, the texts from the Qumran library and early apocryphal and pseudepigraphic texts all expand on Biblical terminology, delineating new supernatural figures. Familiar sons of heaven (1 Enoch 6:2; 13:8; 14:3) and אלים: "gods" (*War Scroll* (*1QM*) 1:10; 14:15; 17:7; Hymns (*1QH*) 10:8) are joined by watchers (Jub 4:15, 21.; 1 Enoch 1:4; Test of the XII Pat 1:5; 8:3) and spirits (Jub 15:31; 2 Macc 3:24). These are joined by the angel of death, rulers of the cosmos (John 12:31; Eph 2:2), figures allied with specific nations and, the area of greatest development, endless daimons and angels with specific names such as Michael, Raphael, Gabriel, Raziel, and Samiel. Keeping track of all the angels and daimons, knowing their names and their roles had become a formidable task.

Late antique writers puzzled over the rise of such rich angelology and daimonology. The rabbis, alert to the gulf between the few named angels in the Bible and the much richer angelology of their day, posited that the Jews brought the names of angels back from Babylonia (jRH 1.2; *GenRab* 48). Modern scholars repeat this theory, since some of the angel names used in the first centuries closely parallel Babylonian angel names and roles (Kohut 1866). This explanation is not sufficient. Where the names come from does not explain why they were borrowed and continued to have importance. That is, had daimons not assumed such a central role in the cosmology at that time, there would have been no reason to borrow names for them. The expanded angelology does clarify and fill in the gaps of obscure Biblical texts (Olyan 1993). But we have to ask what it was about the historical setting that made these types of embellishments plausible and meaningful.

A preliminary and modest goal is to outline some of the main contours of thought which accompanied the increasing interest in angels and daimons. Late antique religious traditions were based on textual themes which were centuries old, many of them dating back to the Ancient Near Eastern religions (J. Z. Smith 1979). The cosmology of these ancient religions, a positively evaluated three-tiered structure of heaven above, earth in the middle, and the underworld beneath, is labeled "locative" due to its emphasis on knowing one's place in the cosmic hierarchy and abiding by it (J. Z. Smith 1978b).

By the third century BCE this view was supplemented by a newer picture in which the earth was conceived as a sphere which hung suspended in the middle of a many layered cosmos, a theme elaborated already in the Greek writer Eudoxus (390–340 BCE) and mirrored in endless subsequent Greco-Roman, Jewish and Christian texts. Here the old visions were supplemented by talk of multiple heavens, a far-off deity, and escape from earthly existence to an eternal after-life in heaven.[14] Jonathan Smith calls this cosmology "utopian" due to its otherworldly emphasis (1978b: 45).

In broad strokes, Hebrew notions of "national monotheism" seen, for example, in Isaiah, parallel to Greek "philosophical monotheism" in Xenocrates, revised the older, traditional model of one highest deity for each city/nation ruling over a divine council.[15] It was no longer thought appropriate for a deity to talk to, interact with, guide, command and reprimand his followers directly.[16]

The deity was still the focus of certain prayers and was not thought to be so far beyond the realm of humans that he was not involved in their lives. It did mean, as outlined here, that some of the supernatural manifestations on earth which might earlier have been thought to be the work of the deity were now considered the work of angels and daimons. Apuleius reflects mid-second century CE etiquette when he negates the possibility that the Gods themselves sent a dream to Hannibal. "It is not," he claimed, "becoming that the Gods of heaven should condescend to things of this nature" (*deDeoSoc* 7).

In the emerging view humans lived at the center of a gigantic cosmic network of rotating planets and stars. Nilsson summarized the shift in relation to Greek religion, but it also applied to emerging Jewish and Christian religious thought.

> The old cosmology was shattered and the universe expanded dizzily. Earth was at the dead center, surrounded by the atmosphere and the seven spheres each with their heavenly bodies. The moon, Mercury, Venus, Sun, Mars, Jupiter and Saturn all shuttled around the earth, as did the fixed stars that composed the Zodiac.
>
> (1948: 99)

The positive and orderly image of earthly existence, so thoroughly propagandized by the earlier royal and priestly writers in the locative worldview, was supplemented by this new vision of the earth as a negative and confining place. Life on earth was radically different from that in the heaven above. On earth people lived and died, all of existence was in flux and thus inferior; far above earth was the realm of the deity, the realm of the eternal where everything is beyond change. The atmosphere between the far-off eternal realm and the world of human existence was like a vast no-man's land in which all sorts of supernatural beings flourished.

The divine presence no longer dwelt in a Temple. For the prophet Ezekiel the sins of the Israelites caused this relocation; for others it was simply impossible to conceive of a deity who dwelt in a specific locale. Instead the deity was everywhere, with a special cultic abode in the highest reaches of heaven.

The Ancient Near Eastern theological staple that the deity/deities are pleased by and partake of animal sacrifice was rejected throughout the Mediterranean basin. The ancient practice was given numerous new interpretations. A common reinterpretation was that sacrifices were directed at the lower level supernatural figures such as angels and daimons and not at the highest God (LXX Deut 32:17). Henry Chadwick calls the trope that daimons feed on sacrifices "universal" (1965: 146 n.1). According to Porphyry daimons "rejoice in libations, and the savor of sacrifices" (*deAbst* 2.42).[17] Jewish texts also describe the hunger of daimons for sacrifices.[18]

The hereditary priest who watched over the cult lost his domain of expertise and power. Classical prophecy died out as well. The shift from temple to charismatic individual signaled the end of the classical world.[19] More audacious figures emerged, individuals who displayed their special status based on their esoteric knowledge and their ability to put divine power into play. They knew the coveted secrets of creation, the fate of the world and of the people who lived in it. These specialists operated individually or in schools centered around a specific teacher, no longer dependent on the fixed sacred locales of the traditional temples.

The ancient cosmologies with their messenger-angels did not disappear. Biblical texts and traditional Greek texts such as Homer continued to inspire devotion and careful reading. The centuries-old picture of the world was supplemented by the new, often darker, vision. Texts from the first three centuries CE, many of which were exegesis of the earlier texts, reflected complex mixtures of elements from the ancient cosmology combined with the newer visions. Messenger-angels gained importance and operated as distinct individuals who could interact with humans in endlessly varying ways. Humans were much more likely to encounter the divine world via these active figures than by any direct interaction with the deity. Rabbinic interpretations of the book of Esther, for example, inserted roles for angels in the story (*EsthRab* 1.10, 3.12, 3.15, 4.2, 7.13). Angels supplied all the aid to the heroine and their interventions reshaped the story to fit rabbinic concerns. Mirroring the narrative role of the angels and daimons, the vicissitudes of daily life were most likely the result of daimonic activity. Life had to be lived with at least one eye out for them at all times.

Thus we come back to the question of the rise of angelology and daimonology and see that just as a body is needed in a murder mystery, so daimons and angels had crucial roles in making the cosmology of the first centuries operational.

Even as we have met the modest goal of outlining the cosmological imperatives that point to rich complexes of angels and daimons, we are still left with the prior question of why this cosmology arose. Diffusionist theories posit the borrowing of the new cosmology from neighboring cultures (such as the cyclically popular option of Persia). Scientific discoveries may also drive the changing cosmologies, since the shifting worldview articulated with Eudoxus' mathematical description of planetary orbits. Julia Annas, for example, argues that the widespread use of notions of pneuma/spirit by the Hellenistic philosophers was their way of hooking into the prestige of the advancements of empirical medicine (1992).

Whatever the causes for the shifts, endless numbers of daimons and angels populated the cosmos in the first three centuries and interacted with humans in every conceivable way. Rabbis worried that female daimons might lie in wait for men who slept alone (bShab 1516). No woman was likely to approach childbirth without worrying about daimons who might come after her newborn child.

Many different theories about the specific origins of daimons circulated. They could be either souls of the dead (Plato, *Crat* 397e–398c),[20] specifically the dead from the Golden Age (Hesiod, *Works*

122–4), ghosts of the wicked (Josephus, *BJ* 7.185) or ghosts of the unjustly dead (Tertullian, *deAnima* 57). The gods of other people are daimons, according to the Septuagint, offering another theory.[21]

Yet another source for the origin of daimons was found in the widely cited story of the beings borne from the intercourse between the sons of God and the daughters of men described in Genesis 6:1–4. The story was lovingly elaborated to include nefarious roles for daimons as the original bearers of many common ills (1Enoch 6–21). The offspring from these illicit liaisons were neither human nor divine, and hence fit perfectly into the search for a daimon genealogy (Justin, *2Apol* 5).

The tendency in both ancient and modern writers when presented with such rich daimon lore is to try to systematize the data. Plutarch's lucid discussions, for example, summarize state-of-the-art theorizing about daimons in the mid-second century CE.[22] Plutarch collected what he considered to be the most authoritative ideas about daimons from his best sources. His synthesis forms the basis of much modern discussion as well. When Plutarch looked around for possible origins, he included Thrace, Egypt and Persia; modern scholars have repeated all of these options.[23]

Plutarch did not even consider the possibility that the contemporary daimonology was Greek in origin, despite the fact that the term "daimon" appears in older Greek texts. Homer, for example, used the term daimon indistinguishably from the term for god (*theos*).[24] Both referred to a type of divine power with no distinct form, no personal history, and no parentage or ancestry (Brenk 1986: 2081). Homer's usage was a far cry from the complex daimonology which confronted Plutarch centuries later.

By Plutarch's time the intermediary role of daimons had received extensive elaboration. Plutarch found particularly useful Plato's statement that daimons are intermediaries between gods and men.[25] This role was familiar from older Greek stories, just as it was from Biblical stories. Plutarch also used Xenocrates' treatise *Epinomis* which organized and explained the hierarchy of gods and daimons more clearly than Plato had done.[26] Just as Plato posits matter and nature as the underlying basis of all existence, for Plutarch daimons are fundamental components of the cosmic hierarchy (*DeDefectu* 10). Souls can work their way up the ladder, and with sufficient purification, become totally divine. Less fortunate souls fall farther down the scale into mortality. Daimons are a structural necessity since they are the "interpretative and ministering nature" between gods and humans (*DeDefectu* 13). Their existence offers explanations for all questionable rites such as eating raw flesh and human sacrifice, actions which were never done on behalf of the higher gods (*DeDefectu* 14). So, too, all questionable stories about gods are really just stories about daimons. The exact distinction between daimons and greater gods is a subject for debate; daimons die, but some, such as the Stoics, argue that only one god is truly eternal (*DeDefectu* 19).

The intermediary roles of daimons were a cliché since these roles reflected so closely the cosmology.[27] Apuleius, a mid-second century CE philosopher, explained that there

> are certain divine powers of a middle nature, sinuate in this interval of the air between highest ether and earth below, through whom our aspirations and our deserts are conveyed to the Gods. The Greeks call them "daimons".
>
> (*deDeoSoc* 6)[28]

Numerous authors besides these attempted to systematize the endless angels and daimons, presenting them in specific ranks and modes of organization, often with military motifs. Sometimes the ranks were simply lists of names while in other cases they included the special tasks of each type of angels. These descriptions varied from author to author. The neo-Platonist Proclus described the ranks and tasks of angels who were arrayed under specific gods.[29] Apollo, for example, was the supervisor of prophetic, musical, and healing angels.[30] The Hebrew text *The Book of Secrets* outlines the names and tasks of the angels arrayed in the first six of the seven heavens under their angelic leaders.[31]

Despite all the attempts by ancient authors to systematize a "daimonology," conceptions of daimons varied widely even within the writings of one author. All these figures were tools of the ancient imagination used to organize, filter, and explain relationships between daily life and the supernatural world. The particular conceptualization depended on the type of text an author was writing and the specific points he was trying to make.

Since the gods were thought to be "entirely different from men" (Apuleius, *deDeoSoc* 7) they were not good tools of the imagination for thinking about the similarities between humans and divine beings. Daimons, on the other hand, share many human characteristics: they have gender, personalities, special interests and abilities. As plastic forces daimons could be utilized in an endless variety of speculations.

Apuleius speculated on daimons and offered more than one theory at the same time (*deDeoSoc* 9). He said that while in the human body, the human soul could be called a daimon, as in the famous case of Socrates' "genius." The human soul after death could be a daimon too. There was yet another type of daimon who was forever free from having a body and possessed special power of "another nature." These were referred to as "Sleep," "Love," etc.

Even as simple a question as whether or not daimons have bodies offered much opportunity for speculation and human/divine comparison. Daimons are like angels in that they have wings, fly from one end of the earth to another, and have foreknowledge of events but also like humans in that they eat, drink and propagate (bHag 16a). Daimons might be described as having bodies of innumerable forms (bBer 6a). If the appearance of daimons looks to humans as if they cast a shadow, then what daimons teach us is that appearances are deceiving (bYeb 122a). They have a nature which is not as sluggish as terrestrial beings, but not as light as ethereal beings (Apuleius, *deDeoSoc* 7).

The personalities were also conceived of as variations on familiar human traits, reminiscent of earlier portrayals of the Greek gods and narrative depictions of the Israelite deity. Daimons exhibit human passions, which makes them much more interesting to us. If their rites are neglected, they are likely to become jealous (Porphyry, *deAbst* 2.37). And they are ambitious, instituting false worship "for they wish to be considered as God and the power which presides over them is ambitious to appear to be the greatest God" (*deAbst* 2.42).

In the end no single picture of daimons emerges even in one writer. As mentioned above in relation to Augustine, with the rise of Christianity daimons became more clearly identified as evil forces. Their roles as disrupters of the cosmic order also become more dramatic as daimons came to bear more of the weight of responsibility for evil in the unfolding Christian theology (Wey 1957).

Life with daimons was as close as with one's neighbours. They could be employed by those who know how to put them to work. The most intimate interactions were imagined, such as sexual intercourse with daimons.[32] Given the opportunity, a daimon would take up residence in a human body. If this happened, the remedy would involve a cosmic battle. We turn now to two such battles, one Christian and the other from a Jewish-influenced ritual preserved in a Greek text.

Daimons, possession and exorcism

In the popular movie *Men in Black,* an intergalactic alien is apprehended when he tries to sneak over the United States border with a group of illegal human aliens. His true identity is revealed when he is unable to answer questions in Spanish. In the first centuries CE a supernatural "alien" spirit could take up residence in a human body only to be unmasked by making an ancient *faux pas*. Just as only the Men in Black can recognize an alien hidden in a human body (though we in the audience get lots of hints), cunning and knowledgeable daimon experts were required to combat late antique daimons. Hollywood's specialists dress in black suits, armed with a fantasy array of secret weapons. In the first centuries in order to unmask a daimon and drive it from someone's body the officiant himself had to have more-than-human status.

While superficially similar, exorcisms in different cultural contexts demonstrate the culturally specific ways in which the interactions between human and supernatural figures are conceived. The conceptions of self and body which underlie an exorcism will differ from setting to setting. Janice Boddy warns us that the conception of self that underlies Zar possession in North Africa is distinct from Western notions (1989). Thus, in turn, surface similarities between, for example, the hysterical woman and the woman possessed in the Zar cult may conceal fundamental differences in the role of the exorcistic rituals. When notions of the "self" are already highly identified with the community, and in turn with idealized notions of femininity, as in the Zar culture, possession takes on different contours than in cases with highly developed notions of self as found in the West. In the case of the Zar cult the woman must learn through the exorcism not to deny her sense of otherness, but exactly the opposite, to increase her sense of control over aspects of her being.

Signs of possession are also culturally diverse, from not laughing to using inappropriate language and gestures.[33] Sometimes demons are put "in place" by comically belittling them and in turn gaining control over the fears associated with them (Kapferer 1979).

Late antique models of exorcism are distinct even from earlier Greek human/divine interactions, even though they also included models of possession (W. O. Smith 1965). In earlier ages the divine spirits controlled humans not by invading their bodies but by affecting their emotions more indirectly. Some types of daimonic possession were also familiar from ancient Semitic traditions, though again it is not clear if the underlying model is the same as that found in the first centuries CE.[34]

The primary model of exorcism, which was the "Late Antique drama *par excellence*,"[35] was based on a deep-seated suspicion of the body. The equation of the body with evil forces arose as the "utopian" model spread in the Greco-Roman world and thus among Jews as well. It was later adopted enthusiastically by Christians. The older notion that the body was part of the natural world which was essentially good was supplemented by concern that the body confined and constrained the soul. Even the rabbis, who rejected celibacy and had a role for highly-regulated sex in marriage, were profoundly anxious about the body (Boyarin 1993: 197–225). As in so many cultures, controlling the body was in part implemented by controlling female bodies.

Our central concern is not to condemn the negative evaluation of the body, an attitude that differs from modern discourse about bodies, or to try to apologize for it.[36] Instead we need to understand the intense focus on the human body which it entailed.

The *Community Rule* (*1QS*), from the library found at the Qumran, offers a rich example of the developing focus on the body.[37] While law was an ancient component of the Israelite worldview, the types of activities legislated in the text are strikingly new. It is hard to envisage them as being of interest to the ancient legislators with a locative view of the world. Interrupting a companion while speaking (7.10), gesticulating with the left hand (7.16), falling asleep during an assembly (7.11), and guffawing foolishly (7.15) – all these actions are subject to punishment.

The code implies that people should be able to control their bodies in such a way as to eliminate any spontaneous behavior. If each individual cannot accomplish this on his own, the rulebook will help him learn to do so. The code itself will make him aware of bodily actions usually done without thinking and without intention. The body must be controlled entirely in order for it not to be a threat. These regulations are in a code which already imagines a community devoid of women, eliminating the special threat of female bodies. The male bodies needed still further control in order to be part of the holy community and have access to holy rites.

Not every text was as extreme, but by the first century CE controlling and escaping the body had become a model for escaping the evils of earthly existence. Human bodies were inseparable from human passions, which were liable to lead individuals astray. Controlling the body was a means of controlling all the evils of bodily existence.

Since controlling the body was so important, in the first centuries any type of spontaneous and unwilled bodily gesture might be a sign of possession by a hostile being. Signs of daimonic possession in the New Testament include falling into fire and water (Matt 17:15), convulsions (Mark 1:26; 9:20; Luke 4:35), foaming at the mouth (Luke 9:39), raving (Mark 5:6), grinding of teeth (Mark 9:18), or showing great fierceness and abnormal strength (Matt 8:28; Mark 5:4; Luke 8:29). Acting in a crazy or insane manner was also evidence of possession (John 8:48; 10:20).

The standard vocabulary of exorcism emerged in the first centuries CE (Kotansky 1995). The first extant uses of the verb ἐξορκίδζω: "drive out (by oath)" and the noun "exorcist" both appear in the writings of the mid-second century satirist Lucian. In one of his satires Lucian described a Syrian exorcist famed for his power over spirits. The exorcist claimed to heal possessed individuals by directly questioning the spirits who make people foam at the mouth and fall down in the moonlight (*Lover of Lies* 16).

Lucian mocked the entire procedure. Skeptical of the proceedings, one of the characters comments ironically that daimons are just about as visible as Platonic forms. Another unflattering portrait by Lucian of an exorcist, preserved only in fragmentary form, refers to the stinking mouth of the exorcist (*AnthPal* 11.427).

The term "exorcist" also appears in an astrological text, *Astrological Influences,* written by Ptolemy in the second half of the second century. Ptolemy explained that in certain phases the planets produce "persons inspired by the gods, interpreters of dreams and exorcists" (14.4). The term is listed as one of several types of experts on divine matters and appears to need no explanation.

The Book of Acts includes the earliest extant Christian use of the term "exorcist" in a striking story about itinerant Jewish exorcists (Acts 19:11–16). This usage is perhaps somewhat earlier than the first appearances in Greco-Roman texts.[38] Seven brothers, described as sons of the chief priest, try to perform an exorcism using Jesus' name. They attempt to drive out the daimon with a common formula of adjuration "I adjure you by . . ."[39] The spirit turns back on them and taunts them "Jesus I recognize, and Paul I know, but who are you?" Their attempt fails and they are driven naked out of the house of the possessed man.

In contrast Paul's healings, mentioned in the previous verses, are presented as miracles coming from the deity via Paul. Even the cloth he touched is effective in healings (Acts 19:11–12). The Jewish exorcists used only the divine name "Jesus", one that might appear to be an odd choice for Jews. As unlikely as this seems, a Jewish-influenced exorcism discussed below includes an adjuration of daimons by the "God of the Hebrews, Jesus."

In Acts the emphasis is not on the daimon, but on the all-too-human exorcists. These figures were of high status, identified as sons of the Jewish chief priest Sceva. No chief priest by that name is known from other sources and even the title is suspect; the import of the name was as a way of referring to a high ranked, cultic Jewish figure. Josephus tells us about a contemporary named Eleazar who did exorcisms using techniques associated with Solomon (*Ant* 8.46–9). Eleazar's claim to authority is not noted, other than the fact that he had access to ancient wisdom. The story from Acts, in contrast, is about high-ranking Jewish ritual failure. This, as it were, reverse exorcism leads not to getting rid of daimons but instead to a supernatural expulsion of the would-be-exorcists. While other New Testament exorcisms reveal the heavenly status of the individual carrying it out,[40] here the story reveals the human status of the exorcists. The priests turn out to be fully human and they themselves are subjected to supernatural control. The point is the same, since it is in the context of the exorcism that we are able to for a moment to see the truth about exactly who is a supernatural power and who is not.

The anecdote from Acts is very compressed, presupposing a familiarity by the reader with more detailed exorcism stories. From other stories in the New Testament, Greco-Roman and rabbinic texts we can reconstruct a fairly standard repertoire of exorcistic techniques. These included looking upwards, sighing or groaning,[41] making hand gestures (such as making the sign of the cross), spitting, invoking the deity and speaking "nonsense" words or letter strings.[42] Sometimes the daimon was commanded to speak as a way of demonstrating both his presence in the human body and the practitioner's control over him.

Use of divine names in rituals, including exorcisms, is an immense topic. The efficacy of names is a sub-set of the general ability of words to have effects on their contexts of use; it is a mistake to see the use of names as qualitatively distinct from other effective uses of words. Promises, legal formulas, namings, and religious formulas such as "I now pronounce you man and wife" are all examples of uses of words to "do things."[43]

Socially conceived effects of language on the contexts of use are culture-specific. Legal and religious formulas, for example, do not translate easily from culture to culture. Great care must be taken in finding out the specific notions by which words are socially understood to have contextual implications.[44] Texts from the first three centuries include a wide variety of ideas, some quite old, about effective and unusual language uses that had implications for rituals. Gods, or daimons, might speak a distinct language which may or may not be comprehensible by humans; inspired speech might also sound like nonsense to humans.[45]

Already in the fourth century BCE a group of words referred to as the Ephesian Letters were used on tablets and rings: ἄσκιον; κατάκιον; λίξ; τετράξ; δαμναμενεύςαἴσια.[46] Athenaeus preserves for us Anaxlas' fourth century BCE unflattering picture of a country snob who wears the letters engraved on little bits of leather (*Deip* 12.548). Their special relationship to exorcisms is evident in Plutarch's disparaging association of them with "magi" who tell people to recite the words over themselves in order to get rid of daimons (*QuesCon* 7.5).

The origin of these words was unknown in antiquity, though there are many theories. Given their murky origins, explanations of their efficacy probably varied with different ancient authors. Common tropes in late antiquity for the power of letter-strings included that they were foreign words, divine names or the names of daimons. As daimon names, for example, they were ready for use to control and exorcise any wayward daimon. Clement of Alexandria believed that they had symbolic import (*Strom* 5.8).

The names of divine beings, including gods, angels and daimons, were thought to have special roles. Divine names did not merely refer to the objects (beings) they named; instead they were direct manifestations of the divine forces. They function similarly to signatures and signature guarantees in our culture, which are understood to be legally binding representations. In modern terminology, their function is not based on their semantics, that is, their reference to some specific object or idea but instead on their relationship to the contexts of use. Each utterance of a divine name activates that force within the ritual, supplying the power to make the ritual effective. These ideas were particularly important in rabbinic traditions where the divine name was understood to be the creative and ordering word *par excellence* (Janowitz 2001).

Jesus is presented in the New Testament as being able to drive out a daimon by speaking a single word (Matt 8:16).[47] His ability to speak in this effective manner is an index of his power. His disciples drive out daimons using Jesus' name, which was widely recognized in Jewish and Christian circles as having special power.[48] In a rabbinic exorcism Rabbi Simon ben Yohai meets a daimon on the road who later possesses a member of the Emperor's family. The rabbi is able to exorcise the daimon simply by uttering his name and telling him to depart (bMeil 17b).[49]

The phrase "Jesus, God of the Hebrews," as mentioned above, occurs in an exorcism text from the set of Greek papyri referred to in modern scholarship as *Greek Magical Papyri* (*PGM*) (4.3007–86).[50] Here we find not a condensed reference to a failed rite as in Acts, but a detailed outline of how to carry out a successful one. The exorcism is structured as follows:

1 Opening instructions:

> A tested charm of Pibechis for those possessed by daimons. Take oil of unripe olives with the herb mastigia and the fruit pulp of the lotus, and boil them with colorless marjoram while saying, "IOEL . . . come out from NN."

2 Instruction for making an amulet:

> The phylactery: On a tin lamella write "IAEO. . . . " And hang it on the patient . . . place [the patient] opposite you, adjure . . .

3 A verbal formula for recitation:

> This is the adjuration: I adjure you by the God of the Hebrews, Jesus IABA . . . who appears in fire . . .
>
> I adjure you by the one who appeared to Osrael in a shining pillar and a cloud by night who saved his people from the Pharaoh [list of additional wonders]
>
> I adjure you by the seal which Solomon placed on the tongue of Jeremiah [long list of more wonders by the deity]

4 Closing instructions:

> And I adjure you, the one who receives this adjuration, not to eat pork, and every spirit and daimon, whatever sort it maybe, will be subject to you. And while adjuring, blow once, blowing air from the tips of the feet up to the face, and it will be assigned. Keep yourself pure, for this charm is Hebraic and is preserved among pure men.

The exorcism is attributed to an Egyptian wonder-worker named Pibechus, meaning falcon. The *Greek Magical Papyri* are replete with Egyptian deities such as the sun god Amon, Osiris, the jackal-headed god of mummification Anubis, and Thoth, the Egyptian god of wisdom often associated with Hermes. References to these gods, their priests, animals associated with Egyptian religious practice and hieroglyphics are all means of incorporating the ancient, secret and powerful traditions of Egypt. The papyrus itself, we must remember, was found in Egypt, preserved due to the favorable weather conditions.

In this particular exorcism there are few obviously Egyptian elements in the rest of the rite beyond the reference to Pibechus. The rite shows several other signs of being a composite of more than one exorcism, perhaps one of which was Jewish.[51] The complex of actions places us squarely in the realm of a ritual expert, with a great disparity between the knowledge demanded of the one doing the exorcism versus the one who is possessed. The casual reader of the papyrus would find much of the text technical and obscure, requiring extensive knowledge of the animal and vegetable world as well as knowledge about daimons and their roles.

The first section produces a concoction, which presumably was applied to the patient. Anointing sick people with olive oil or herbal mixtures was a widespread practice. In this case a complex mixture is created which itself requires both mixing ingredients and knowing formulas to say over them. The insertion of the patient's name in the formula is followed by "etc." implying that the practitioner must know enough to complete the rite on his own.

Herbs were thought to be particularly effective in drawing out daimons, in addition to the numerous other roles they played in healing. The herbs themselves might have been gathered with the recitation of a special formula such as found elsewhere in the papyri (*PGM* 4.286–95). Josephus mentioned a root named Baaras after the ravine where it is found. This root, which had to be extracted with great care due to its lethal potency, was used in exorcisms. It expelled daimons when used on an afflicted person (*BJ* 7.180–5). So too the rabbis ruled that it is permissible to wear an amulet on the Sabbath that contains writings or herbs (jShab 6.2).

The construction and use of amulets (section 2) was widespread in the first centuries and will be discussed at greater length in the next chapter.[52] The amulet produced for this exorcism comes with its own guarantee; it is of the type, which is "terrifying to every daimon, a thing he fears" (3017–18).

Section 3 of the rite incorporates the power of divine names, as discussed above. In this exorcism divine names appear in both the easily recognizable form, such as Jesus, and as strings of letters. The letter strings alternate with short descriptions of the deity's actions, one of which describes the creation of the daimon in "holy paradise." Since the deity made the daimon, he should be able to re-assert his control over the wayward being.

This section also contains a long list of wonders which are a mini-summary of Israelite history (historiola).[53] The summary simultaneously establishes the power of the deity who stands behind the exorcist and the genealogy of the exorcist himself. Each story of divine aid given in the past makes it more likely that divine aid will come again, shifting the historical precedents into the present episode. A similar goal is reached in Navaho healing ceremonies via elaborate sand paintings depicting mythical themes, each one constructed specifically for a certain rite. The patient then sits in the middle of the painting, literally embedding his or her personal story directly into the myth portrayed in the sand painting (Gill 1981).

In a Christian-influenced Mayan exorcism recorded recently in the Yucatan the altar is transformed from an everyday shelf into a place where the spirits appear (Hanks 1996: 184). The officiant calls upon the earth spirits to come and force out the winds which are harming the patient from the area of the altar. In contrast, in just the same way the body of the beneficiary is swept clean of the winds. In our late antique exorcism the contested space is the patient's body. He is not brought into contact with sacred space in order to focus divine power on him. Instead it is the divine power manifest in the person of the exorcist which "sweeps clean" the daimon. The daimon may only be banished as far as the next body. Often this is a human body since daimons are looking for human bodies to use as homes.

The Mayan healing ceremony effects "the production and transformation of lived space," by "creating a universal space." The story of the specific patient is universalized and the universal spirits make a particular appearance in the rite. In the Pibechus exorcism we see a similar universalizing of the patient's story, as it is placed within the history of the Israelite deity, and a particularizing of the deity's story by manifesting his power for the benefit of the specific patient. The rite itself also transforms the setting. The participation of the supernatural power is manifested by the use of the third person (the One who . . .) just as in the Mayan exorcism.

The exorcist employs the seal of Solomon, that is, a ring with the seal of Solomon on it (section 4). As daimon lore grew in the first centuries, a vast part of it was associated with Solomon and his seal. The brief Biblical reference to Solomon's great wisdom, his proverbs and songs and his knowledge of plants and animals (1 Kings 4:29–34) was expanded to include his encyclopedic knowledge of astrology, the power of roots and the forces of spirits (Wis 7:15–22). An entire text, *The Testament of Solomon*, recounts Solomon's power over the daimons as he puts them to work at building the Temple.

While the deity ruled the world, Solomon ruled the world of daimons (*ApocAdam* 7.13) and inherited special exorcistic music from David (Ps-Philo, *LiberAntBib* 60).[54] References to Solomon and his powers over daimons decorate amulets,[55] door lintels,[56] and ceramic amulet bowls buried outside houses.[57] Numerous Christian writers such as Origen (*ComMatt* 23.110; *PG* 13, col 1757) and "On the Origin of the World" (*NHC* II, 5.107,3) from the Christian library found at Nag Hammadi refer to Solomon and his power over daimons.

The rabbis repeat the trope as well, describing Solomon's power over beasts and birds (Targum Sheni to Esther).[58] Later tradition attributes the Book of Healings destroyed by Hezekiah to Solomon (jBer 10a, bPes 56a; Duling 1975: 16). Solomon was often pitted against Asmodeaus, known in rabbinic literature as the "king of daimons."[59]

Exorcism stories from the first centuries are replete with references to Solomon's mysterious ring. It was presumed to have been passed down through the generations to contemporary wise men. The ring accrued to itself the power of these generations of men who employed it, as well as the initial power it received from Solomon. Josephus described an exorcist named Eleazar who held a ring under the nose of the possessed person while reciting Solomon's name (Josephus, *Ant* 8.46–9). According to a rabbinic story the ring had the name of God written on it, not at all surprising given the centrality of the divine name in Judaism.[60] Early Christian pilgrims were told that St Sylvia was able to see Solomon's ring among the relics which the church owned.[61]

Solomon is not invoked often in the *PGM* which contain many classical names such as Aphrodite and Artemis (M. Smith 1979: 133). Many more references to Solomon are found on the numerous gemstones extant from late antiquity. These precious and semi-precious stones, engraved with a stereotyped mode of decorations, were worn as amulets. They invoke primarily Egyptian and Jewish names (M. Smith 1979: 133). Their particular vocabulary of decoration (lion-headed serpent, "attacked" eye) appears to be distinct from the references to stones in the Greek papyri. The surprisingly strict divide between the gemstones used for curing digestion, gout and aching back and the references to stones in the *PGM* is valuable evidence of the specialization of esoteric knowledge. Solomon and his seal were so famous that he is a crossover figure, appearing in both the *PGM* and on the gems.

The closing of the text clearly identifies it with Hebrews and Hebrew traditions, as does the historiola and many of the divine names. The references are sometimes distorted, or based on stereotypes as in the references to not eating pork and staying pure, as if the editor had limited direct knowledge of Jewish traditions.

Decades ago Knox argued that the text could have been employed in synagogues.[62] The Pibechus rite as preserved, however, is part of an extensive collection of rituals edited in Greco-Roman circles but not Jewish ones (unlike *The Book of Secrets* discussed in the next chapter). These references point us to the international reputation of the Hebrews/Jews for secret wisdom (Chapter 1). The ritual combines two of the great stereotypes from the first centuries: the centrality of both Hebrews and Egypt as sources of powerful wisdom.

The Pibechus exorcism contrasts with the exorcism of the daimon Asmodeus described in the wry novel *Tobit*, often presented as the first Jewish possession story.[63] In this novel, which pokes fun at all the characters, a pious man from Judah named Tobit is blinded when bird-droppings fall into his eyes while he naps under a tree. His regular religious activities, including zealous burial of neglected corpses, do not protect him from this humiliating calamity. He is rescued through the help of the angel Raphael, who, disguised as a fellow traveler, helps Tobit's son to procure a fish whose entrails cure his blindness and furthermore smoke out a daimon who has been haunting his daughter-in-law-to-be's bridal chamber. The exorcism in Tobit is a modified sacrifice.[64] Reversing the "pleasing odor" of the Biblical sacrifices, the odor of the fish's liver and heart drives off the daimon before he can make the new bridegroom his eighth victim.

The papyrus exorcism is a highly professionalized version that seems far removed from the simple story in *Tobit*. The human exorcist, who procures the items he needs based on his training (and the written instructions he uses), has displaced the divine intervention represented by the angel. The entire procedure is more elaborate, especially the verbal formulas. We find few exorcisms from the first centuries CE that have no verbal formulas at all, as in *Tobit*. The war of words between the exorcist and the daimon is too central.

The *Tobit* exorcism still has links with the older locative worldview. The daimon has to be driven off from human society, bound by Raphael so that he can never return to bother humans again. In both our examples of exorcism rituals the supernatural forces gathered to combat the daimon had to outweigh its power, either by the power of a divine name alone or by the rite which combined an amulet with the recitation of stories of divine power. The human world exists in the sphere of the daimons and their natural homes are in human bodies. In this finely calibrated fight the true status of each combatant is revealed only in the battle itself. Our examples of exorcism are presented as daring attempts to tear off disguises and show the world as it really is. In the process of the exorcism itself, a human is brought once more within the protecting realm of the good supernatural powers, but not without effort.

The focus on bodies that marked the first centuries leads us to expect an emphasis on exorcism. That is, stories of exorcism lead us inexorably to bodies. "[T]he very notion of possession," Janice Boddy reminds us, "indicates from the outset that the body is the locus of negotiation between the spirits and the initiate and of the redefinition of her identity" (1989: 89).

With the rise of the utopian worldview, the human body gained prominence as the battleground for conflicts between human and supernatural forces. Evil forces were so closely intertwined with life on earth the war had to be fought one body at a time. It is in this context that baptism came to include an exorcism, marking the body of the new Christian as aligned with Christ.[65] The daimon is not being sent back to his home. Instead, getting rid of the evil force is dependent on a miraculous intervention by the deity, since the human world is the natural place for daimons to lurk. Tremendous effort must be made to intervene. The deity has not so much to retake space that was already his as to manifest his divine power in the midst of the world of the daimonic. The deity and the exorcist are the intruders here since it is natural for human bodies to house daimons.[66] If the exorcist fails, he himself can be driven out, as in the story in Acts, and the reign of the daimonic continues.

Through this whole discussion we are far from the realm of magic, until we find some of these rituals being labeled magic in the modern period. Exorcism was too integral a part of the late antique world to be cast in doubt.[67] A person's body was the finest instrument for gauging just how corrupt the world had become and the battle against evil was fought one body at a time.

3

ANCIENT RITES FOR GAINING LOVERS

Ancient Hebrew instructions for how to cause a woman to fall in love with a man state that the first task is to take two small sheets of tin and write on one the name of a man and on the other the name of a woman, along with a list of angel names. Next follows a prayer for recitation:

> I ask of you, angels who rule the fates of the children of Adam and Eve, that you do my will and bring in conjunction the planet of N son of N into conjunction with (the planet of) the woman N daughter of N. Let him find favor and affection in her eyes and do not let her belong to any man except him.

The tin sheets should then, on the 29th day of the month, be put into a furnace or into a bath frequented by the woman. In order for this procedure to be effective, the practitioner is told to abstain from meat, sexual intercourse, and wine (*The Book of Secrets* [Heb.: *Sefer ha-Razim*] *SHR* 2.31–45).[1]

Another ancient set of instructions for the same purpose, this time written in Greek, begins with a wax or clay model of a man and woman. Secret ingredients are tied on the neck of the female figurine and strings of letters are engraved on each of the woman's limbs. The practitioner then pierces the model, reciting a formula "I pierce her so she will remember only me." Next the practitioner is told to write a formula on a tablet, tie it to the statue with 365 knots, recite a short formula out loud and then bury the statue in the grave of someone untimely or violently dead. The text explains that the secret ingredient tied to the neck of the female figurine comes from the body of a daimon(!), though it is so secret that it cannot even be clearly explained in the text (*PGM* 4.296–466).

These rites, simply put, are shocking to modern sensibilities, and thus distanced from what are thought to be normative religious practices and concerns. The first is from *The Book of Secrets*, which, despite the general demise of the category "magic," is still described by many modern scholars as a classic example of late antique Jewish "magic."[2] Similarly, the second rite is from the *Greek Magical Papyri*. The texts automatically become the work of ancient magicians who lurked at the edge of society trying to avoid representatives of official religion and the law.

Scholars reinforce this interpretation of the social context of the rituals by adding the word "magic" to their translations of the text. Morgan, for example, translates עסק: "practice" as "practice magic" and מעשה: "rite, action" as "magical rite" (1983: 21). Numerous insertions of the word "magic" occur in the recent English translation (Betz 1986) of the Greek papyri as well, such as "magical material" for "material" (4.304), "magical power" for "authority" (1.216), and "magical operation" for "operation" (4.161).

Hebrew terms for magic do not occur *anywhere* in *The Book of Secrets*. In the thousands of lines of papyri the Greek word for magic and its derivatives occur in only a few places: "initiate of sacred magic" (1.126–30), "magical soul" (4.243), "chief of all magicians" (4.2289) and in an injunction that the masses should not practice magic (12.401–7). Some of the phrases, such as "sacred initiate," may draw on the positive connotations associated with the magi we saw, for example, in Clement of Alexandria's writings. They do not warrant associating the mass of rituals with modern notions of magic.

As a starting point for analyzing the love rites, the textual traditions classify the actions as a particular *type* of action. They are referred to in the Hebrew texts as מעשה: "rite, action" and in Greek as πρᾶξις: "rite, action." Rabbinic literature refers to a category of practitioner employing the same term איש מעשה: "man of rite, action." One of the most famous of these practitioners, Honi the Circle-Drawer, was famed for bringing rain by drawing a circle on the ground and reciting prayers.[3] These figures appear to have been in competition with the rabbis, having their own sources of knowledge and power.

In *The Book of Secrets*, the "rites" are explicitly connected with ancient traditions which pre-date even Biblical texts. The opening of the composition describes the text as "a book from the books of secrets" given by the angel Raziel to Noah before he went into the ark.[4] The claim to status as a heavenly book, a pre-flood esoteric tradition revealed only to the few, was a common trope in apocryphal and pseudepigraphic texts.[5] This claim is supplemented by a chain of transmission similar to that found in rabbinic texts (*Avot* 1.1), a step towards the "rabbinization" of the rite traditions. Another step towards incorporating the rites in a rabbinic framework is the inclusion of hymn material in the seventh heaven. These hymns connect the entire text with rabbinic liturgy.

The Greek term πρᾶξις: "rite, action" is a very broad term used in many cultural settings. It often focused on the practical aspects of some endeavor, that is, instructions as opposed to theoretical investigations. In the papyri the term refers to the technical contextual aspects of achieving a particular goal, that is, which items must be used and which words recited in order to achieve success. This does not mean that a "rite" is without any theological underpinnings; only that these will not be discussed under the topic of "rite." The Greek rites are also presented as ancient wisdom, sometimes referred to specifically as "traditional" (*PGM* 1.54) and sometimes connected with ancient figures such as Pythagoras and Democritus (*PGM* 7.795).

Some parts of the rites in the Greek and Hebrew handbooks are identical, such as praying to Helios (*SHR* 4.60; *PGM* 4.247) and making amulets (*SHR* 2.63; *PGM* 4.80). Common goals include knowing the future (*SHR* 5.15; *PGM* 4.3210 and 7.540–78), healing (*SHR* 1.29; *PGM* 7.193–214), talking to or questioning various types of spirits (*SHR* 3.175; *PGM* 7.505–28), and gaining power or influence over enemies and friends (*SHR* 2.18; 2.46 *PGM* 10.24–35; 12.397–400).

The range of goals is quite striking. Serious requests for healing occur next to the seemingly comic, such as one recipe promising to fill a room up with smoke in order to impress friends. Rites to make the practitioner immortal are juxtaposed with attempts to avoid getting drunk.[6]

Reading through the texts is often bewildering. The rituals appear to be in no particular order. They combine dense sets of instructions with long lists of angel names. Numerous objects are mentioned ranging from the familiar (flour, incense) to the more exotic (ashes from an idol, lion's heart). *The Book of Secrets* does have a clear structure based on the model of seven heavens. The first six levels outline the placement of the angelic camps in that level, the names of the angels, the tasks over which they are appointed, and how the angels can be employed. The seventh and final heaven contains only hymns praising the deity.

The Greek handbooks do not have any clear overall organization. They mirror most closely the arrangement of rites *within* the individual heavens of *The Book of Secrets* where similar themes reappear in various sections with no clear organization.[7] Emendations, variants, and multiple copies of the same rite demonstrate the status of the papyri as ancient working documents (Nock 1972: 178–9). *The Book of Secrets* is somewhat cleaner, but strikingly similar.

Assigning a precise date to these handbooks and the rituals they contain is difficult. Dating *The Book of Secrets* depends on a single reference to the Roman indiction ("the fifteen year cycle of the reckoning of the Greek kings") in 1.27–8. This system was instituted in 312 CE, though not used for non-fiscal concerns until the second half of the fourth century (Margalioth 1966: 24–5).[8] The reference dates only the final editing of the handbook; it probably contains rituals from a much earlier period. The bulk of the Greek papyri included in the collection date from the fourth century. Here again they include earlier material such as short compositions which date to the second century (Nock 1972: 176).

All of the rites in *The Book of Secrets* employ angels as helpers. Angels of silence are asked to help silence powerful people (2.20) and angels of fire help extinguish a fire (3.29). Most of the Greek texts also employ helpers, referred to by the term παρεδρος: "assistant." Morton Smith estimated that 70 per cent of the *PGM* employ such helpers (1986: 68).

Given the centrality of these helpers, the key to success in these rites is getting the assistants to do their jobs. Verbal formulas direct the assistants. Many of the formulas are adjurations which use first person singular forms of משׁביע: "adjure, swear" and ὁρκίζω: "adjure, swear."[9] Adjurations are a form of swearing or oath-taking, distinct because they implicate the individual toward whom the adjuration is directed and not the one making the adjuration. Adjuring was a common practice in the first centuries. Pliny remarks that people adjure the gods before any dangerous undertaking (*NH* 28.4). A specific adjuration might invoke a deity[10] or simply refer in general to "Name."[11] Jews who were reluctant to use adjurations could attain the same social goal by taking an oath that would make them into liars if the angels did not fulfill the requests.[12]

Adjurations appear frequently on amulets, as for example, "I adjure you, the spirit of the bones" (Naveh and Shaked 1985, amulet no. 1) and "I adjure against Marten daughter of Qoriel" (amulet no. 8). They also occur on the clay bowls buried near houses as protective amulets, with formulas such as "I adjure you, I adjure you in the name of he who is great" (bowl no. 6).[13]

Adjurations were so common that they appear in rabbinic stories without attracting any attention. We hear, for example, of R. Joshua b. Levi adjuring the angel of death (bKet 77b).[14] When the angel gives him a cosmic tour which permits him a premature glimpse of paradise, the rabbi jumps down into paradise and refuses to go back to earth and die. He adjures the angel so that the angel will not be able to take him back. As always in rabbinic stories, the point of the story is about something else (in this case the importance of fulfilling one's vows); the reference to the adjuring of the angel is off-hand and without controversy. The context here is of a struggle between near equals, a battle of wits and words in which the rabbi can overcome the natural order (die first, then paradise) if his oath against the angel works.

Adjuring angels, as an extension of oaths, is a mode of legal discourse – an unusual mode perhaps since one party is supernatural. The officiant is trying to make the angel comply with a demand based on common social practices for bringing about compliance. Angels are implicated in the legal structures of the general society, now extended to the supernatural level. The thrust of the formulas is to put the angels in a situation in which they cannot refuse to help the person making the request. They can no more pretend that they did not hear the request than someone can ignore a summons.

Just as arguing before the Supreme Court requires a special kind of training, adjurations in these ritual handbooks reflect specialized training. The officiant needs to have encyclopedic knowledge of where angels/daimons live, what their roles are, their regular and secret names, which items are related to them and how their names reflect their spheres of activity. All of this esoteric knowledge reinforces the legal formulas since it heightens the practitioner's status as an expert.

Neither of the love-binding formulas described above includes the specific verbs of adjuration. They are constructed using formulas familiar from other ritual settings. Christopher Faraone delineates four types of formulas found on *defixiones*, small sheets of metal engraved with binding formulas and then placed in tombs or wells (1991). The first type of formula Faraone calls a direct binding formula, as seen in "I bind NN." The Greek rite described above uses a similar phrasing: "I pierce her." No direct binding formulas appear in *The Book of Secrets* since so many of the rites are directed at angels.

The second type of formula Faraone calls a "prayer formula," since it asks the gods or daimons to undertake an action on behalf of the speaker. This is the type of formula found in the Hebrew love rite: "I ask of you, angels who rule the fates of the children of Adam and Eve." This is a minority phrasing in the text and is cast in politer terms than the adjurations. The third type of formula described by Faraone is a "wish" formula, such as "May NN be unsuccessful." This phrasing obscures the agent, leaving it ambiguous as to who exactly is harming the victim. This type of formula is not found in *The Book of Secrets* since it does not include the use of an angelic assistant.

Faraone's fourth and final form is a "similibus" formula. Here the speaker uses a persuasive analogy such as "As this corpse is cold and lifeless, in the same way may NN become cold and lifeless." This last category does not appeal to any power but is based on a passive formulation. We do find a similar formulation in one section "Just as a woman will return to the infant of her womb, so this N will return to me to love me from this day" (1.146). The recipes in *The Book of Secrets* are usually cast in more active formulations, though many of them do use analogies. Most importantly, since the various formulas appear in the midst of a majority of adjurations they assimilate to adjurations and it is easy to read them without noting their distinct construction.

The Book of Secrets is an implicit guide to the etiquette of late antique request formulas. Requests must be directed to the appropriate supernatural being, and in the appropriate language. None of the prayer formulas are addressed to the main deity, who does not have the task of dealing with the topics addressed in the rites. Nothing is asked directly from the occupant of the seventh heaven; the language of choice in the seventh heaven is praise.

The verbal formulas fill many roles in the rites. In addition to directing the angels, they incorporate the power of divine names into the rite. Sometimes the names may look at first glance like a string of nonsense letters. The string of letters "*KOMPHTHO KOMASITH KOMNOUN,*" for example, is followed by "you who shook and shake the world" (*PGM* 4.1323). Divine names most importantly have reference (to the divine being) and not sense. All divine names, therefore, and especially international divine names, do not have to have any clear meaning. These names, far from being nonsense, directly incorporate the power of the beings addressed into the rite. The Greek rite incorporates the daimons in other ways (using the daimon body parts).

Very few of the rites include only verbal formulas. Numerous, sometimes rather exotic, objects are employed in tandem with the verbal formulas. Some of these objects are employed in the rites based on models of modified sacrifices. As discussed briefly in Chapter 2, the sacrificial cult was increasingly understood in the first three centuries CE to be the purview of daimons and not the highest deity.[15] This was part of the general movement away from traditional animal sacrifice that swept the Mediterranean world in the first centuries CE (J. Z. Smith 1995: 22). Sometimes talk *about* sacrifice replaced animal sacrifice in the well-described shift from Temple to home/house of study. Other times the focus of the sacrificial offering shifted from the main deity to lower-level supernatural beings. The cult was directed at the daimons and angels, attracting or placating supernatural figures just as ancient sacrifices had done for centuries before. Daimons are said to be "riveted" to "burnt-offering" and blood (Origen, *CC* 8.62); they "delight in frankincense and blood and the odors rising from burnt sacrifices" (*CC* 4.32).[16]

> Just as the daemons, sitting by the altars of the Gentiles, used to feed on the steam of sacrifices, so also the angels, allured by the blood of the victims which Israel offered as symbols of spiritual things, and by the smoke of the incense, used to dwell near the altars and to be nourished on food of this sort.
>
> (Origen, *DePr* 1.8.1)

This stunning statement of Origen's was probably borrowed from Jewish reinterpretations of sacrifice traditions.[17] Daimon sacrifices are also mentioned in rabbinic texts, including casting bread into the sea for the daimon known as the Prince of the Sea (שר הים).[18]

Daimon sacrifices were not the full-fledged animal offerings known from the Hebrew Scriptures and early Greek literature. Substitutes of herbs, animal parts, or even rocks were used instead. The altar was a smaller and therefore more portable version of the ancient altars (J. Z. Smith 1995: 26).

The rite might take place in numerous settings, including a private house, the side of a river, near a tomb, or, as in many cases, in a place which is completely unspecified. In all these cases the site is sanctified by the ritual itself (J. Z. Smith 1995: 26).

The Greek rite employs a figurine, as do other rites in *The Book of Secrets*, though not the love rite.[19] These objects are particularly disturbing to modern sentiments. Except for a small sub-set of objects (crosses, menorahs) the material dimensions of ritual are often relegated to the fringes of expression. The most suspect are images of humans, often described as "voodoo" dolls, and statues of gods.

Even in the writings of art historians images are often presented in terms of decoration, and not for their more dramatic cultural roles. Ancient suspicions about images reinforce "the long-standing valorization of the spiritual over material form" (Freedberg 1989: 60). It is all too easy to overlook the fact that, among their many social roles, statues "could detect unchaste men and women, protect one against bugs, avert calamities, and generally perform in a whole variety of beneficent ways" (Freedberg 1989: 92).

Ancient and modern polemics concur on this issue. Hebrew Scriptures connected statues with idolatry and the worship of false gods.[20] These prohibitions divert attention from long-standing traditions of depicting the deity in the form of a bull and members of his entourage in various hybrid animal forms.[21] Greek religious practices included a variety of roles for statues. Prayers were offered to statues; they were bathed, clothed and carried in processions. Even as these practices developed they were critiqued (Xenophanes, DK 21 B 15–16). Roman religious practices included both the use of small statues in family rituals and larger statues in public cults.[22]

In the first three centuries, images were widely employed in rituals. While stereotypes present Jews as eschewing images and Greeks as embracing them, the evidence is more complex. Prayers were offered to statues as they had been in the past (Dionysius of Harlicarnusses 8.56). Sometimes divine presences were invited into statues. Neoplatonic writings describe the placing of herbs and stones inside statues as part of rituals which manifested divine presences.[23] While Biblical polemics against images were repeated in later Jewish texts, the history of Jewish art is richer than expected at every turn. Plants, animals and even images of humans were used in synagogue art, mosaics in public and private settings, on tombs, and on smaller objects such as jewelry.[24]

Jews, Christians and pagans agreed that statues could be animated by supernatural presences. The nature of these presences was subject to debate. Were they really divine presences or simply the tricks of daimons?[25] While not as strident and consistent as the Hebrew Scriptural texts, Greek and Roman texts critiqued the use of statues and presented "barbarian" practices as aniconic and therefore praiseworthy.[26] The tractate *Asclepius* from the *Corpus Hermeticum* warned that daimons may implant themselves in statues as a means of fooling gullible people (24,37). Maximus, who animated a divine statue via hymns in the presence of the young Julian (350s), is called "a theatrical miracle-worker." His mode of operation is contrasted negatively with "purification of the soul which is attained by reason" (Eunapius, *VitaPhil* 475). These critiques may have been fueled by an old anti-iconic stance.

The hostile attitude towards the use of statues was in full force when the nineteenth century definitions of magic were developed.[27] According to James Frazer's famous interpretation of the "voodoo doll," the person using the doll in a magic ritual mistakenly thought that the harm inflicted on the doll was directly mimicked in the intended victim. In this model "magic" is based on the misguided analogical laws of "contagion" (once connected always connected) and "like leads to like" (harming a doll is harming a person).

There is no evidence, however, that people engaged in such actions cannot differentiate between sticking a pin in a doll and harming a person. Most participants would not claim that the simple act of binding a figure *in and of itself* is enough to bind a woman. The analogical actions are embedded in complex rituals, which in turn depended on culturally specific notions of supernatural forces.

A more fruitful way of thinking about the role of figurines in rituals such as the Greek love rites is to begin with the observation that rituals are a very special type of cultural activity. Every ritual act is a copy of a model established by a god or a founding figure of the religious tradition (Parmentier 1994: 128–34). When Israelites rested on the Sabbath, they copied the deity who rested on the very first Sabbath (Gen 2:1–3). The rabbinic celebration of Passover re-enacts an ancient rabbinic retelling of the Exodus story. Every Eucharist is a copy of the model set by Jesus when he instituted the rite, no matter what the particular interpretation of the rite is. Roman sacrifices were traced back to the actions of the founders of Rome, Romulus and Remus, and the first king, Numa.

In each case a ritual recreates in the present actions which happened in the past. The actions themselves are special in that they involve deities or some type of supernatural forces. The divine forces at work in the rituals are presumed to be effective, since the actions in the past were successfully completed. That is, the rituals re-enact the effective past actions of deities. The derivative rites are then successful to the extent that their "excessive formality" harkens back to the action which they copy (Parmentier 1994: 130). In order to be a successful copy of the successful action, the rite must have a clear structure which follows the specific guidelines of the past.

Rituals are models in yet other ways. They include in themselves exact copies of their goals. A marriage ceremony includes in itself a model of a completed model; the vows delineate the perfect marriage. Sometimes the models are created in the midst of the rituals via speech which outlines the model in detail for the participants (honor, love and obey). Sometimes these models are presented via actions and objects, such as the modeling of the destroying of enemies by including an exact model of the act of destroying. They do not represent in an arbitrary manner what it is they stand for; instead they have the *identical* form of what they stand for.[28] A statue, in semiotic terms, is a very special kind of representation of a human since it has the exact same form as a human.

Binding a figure is then a particularly close model of the exact action sought in the love rite. When the model of binding is combined with the formula that includes the person's name, the binding action is directed towards that specific person (and only that specific person). The "standing for" model of binding is formally related to what it stands for at yet another level if it includes an actual piece of what (who) it represents (the person's sweat, hair, nail-clippings etc.).

Amulets, used in numerous settings including the exorcism discussed in the previous chapter, also materially represent divine forces. Hundreds of amulets are preserved from the first centuries, now located in museums and private collections.[29] Millions more no doubt perished due to their small size and the materials they were made out of. Amulets were made out of precious metals, stone, animal parts, vegetable or mineral matter and just about anything else that can be engraved or put in a small sack. They were tied on arms and hands, placed on people's doorposts, hung on animals and buried near houses and buildings. Ancient portraits show them as part of daily attire. Amulets contained Biblical verses, Homeric verses, angel names, incantations, strings of letters, and, sometimes, small drawings.

Amulets predate the first three centuries CE, with thousands found in archaeological digs and others mentioned in literary texts. Aristophanes' *Plutus* describes a man who shrugs off a blackmailer by pointing out that he has a protective ring (883ff.). Biblical verses, including Deuteronomy 6:4–9; 11:13–21 and Exodus 13:10, 11–16, command the Israelites to bind the deity's statutes on their hands and on their foreheads. These verses, and sometimes the Decalogue, as in the examples found at Qumran, were written on small pieces of parchments, placed in small boxes and then bound on hands and on the head.[30] The exact implementation of the verses may have varied in different Jewish communities; the *Letter of Aristeas* refers simply to wearing symbols on one's hands (159).[31]

Wearing or hanging amulets was standard practice among Jews, Christians and Greco-Roman believers in the first centuries.[32] The particular nuance of amulets from this time period is their international flavor, with names and motifs from a variety of traditions and settings. The makers of these objects hoped to draw on all traditions which had the reputations of being powerful and ancient, hence the Egyptian and Jewish elements.

Rabbinic texts discuss numerous types of amulets, including an ornament in the shape of a reptile (tAZ 5.2). In rabbinic circles it was ruled permissible to wear an effective amulet even on the Sabbath (mShab 8:2). Amulets were forbidden to Jews only when they made use of the wrong supernatural powers, such as the amulets mentioned in 2 Maccabees 12:40 which had the names of foreign gods on them.

Amulets are best defined by their use. That is, amulets are any objects used to directly mediate between divine forces and a specific individual or place. They work by bringing some type of physical representation of the supernatural force into direct physical contact with the person/animal/place for which aid is sought. An amulet functions much like a blessing said over a person, only in this case it represents the forces of blessings in material form and physically connects them with the individual.

This physicality of the "blessing" is again a stumbling block, as many modern researchers are more comfortable with spoken prayers than their material representations. As in the case of the figurines, the problem of material objects is that they appear to themselves become the focus of human concern. "Idolatry" is present when the statue/amulet/scroll and not the forces that it represents are thought to heal and protect.

In our love rites the verbal formulas and the use of objects reinforce the presence of the divine forces in the rite in numerous overlapping ways. Angels are called on by name, invoking their presence in the rite. Their names are also literally embedded in the rite by means of the lists of names on the lead tablets. In the Greek love rite, body parts of a daimon are bound onto the statue, a very direct representation of divine force in the rite. The molded image is also put in contact with the supernatural forces when it is placed in the grave. The angels, in turn employ other cosmic forces, using the natural forces of the planets to accomplish their task.

In order for the binding spells to be successful they must be kept a secret from the people towards whom they are directed.[33] In addition, other rites were thought to be so ancient and powerful they could not be divulged to anyone. This theme echoes in the very title of *The Book of Secrets* and in the repeated exhortations against revealing the rites found throughout the *Greek Magical Papyri*.

We noted at the start of the chapter that rites like our love rites are among the last to be freed of the polemical label magic. In terms of goals, mundane concerns such as making a woman fall in love with a man appear too petty or not spiritual enough to be part of religion. So too cursing rituals do not seem to fit into the proper bounds of religion.[34] These are, of course, highly selective notions of religion. Looking for material gain, cursing, condemning and generally thwarting enemies were all part and parcel of ancient religious practices. The intimate and inseparable connection between curses and blessings is demonstrated in the Hebrew Scriptures where the two are a special category of speech. Both types of speech work automatically and cannot be taken back since they have automatic efficacy.[35] If evil could not be cast in the way of others, neither could good.

Once suspect goals are eliminated as a reason for classifying the texts as magic, we are left with the major concern of the methods used in these texts. Any use of a divine image or even a divine name threatens to lead people into thinking that the image or name is the object of veneration in and of itself and not due to its special relationship to the powers it represents. Any of these rites, taken out of their contexts, easily looks like "magic." Once the context is lost, the complex "standing for" relationships that they entail are perforce lost and it looks as if the models themselves are supposed to supply the efficacy and supernatural power.

Just as legal language sounds like nonsense to the uninitiated, people outside of the implicit social contract can intentionally or accidentally malign any of these rites. It is easy to impute that the amulet's user thinks that the amulet itself *really is* the god, and thus to accuse him or her of idolatry or magic.

Freedberg rejects as confusing the attempt to classify all the instances where art has a relationship with its context of use as "magic" (1989: 80). The term has limited explanatory value. So, too, no religions in the first three centuries functioned without some type of physical or material representations of divinity in their rituals, even if, as in the case of the rabbis, it was a name or a scroll. Just as the primordial model of a ritual is present formally in the ritual and the goals as well, so, too, some word or object must have a formal relationship with some divine force, or a ritual would be nonsensical action. Every part of the love rites was carefully constructed to fit into contemporary notions of cause and effect – especially cause and effect where angels, daimons and gods were concerned.

4

USING NATURAL FORCES FOR DIVINE GOALS

Maria the Jewess and early alchemy

In the 1980s the single best word to use when trying to sell just about anything was "natural." This word tapped into the public imagination in such a powerful way that it endorsed everything from food items to shampoo. Notions of "natural" [Gr: φυσικός] were also important in the first three centuries. An entire literature about the forces of nature appears to have emerged in the last centuries BCE, though most of the writings are known to us only in fragmentary form.

We hear, for example, of Bolos of Mendes, author of lost treatises "Natural Forces" and "On Sympathies and Antipathies."[1] Pliny recorded several marvelous tales from Democritus the Naturalist, who appears to have written extensively about the animal world and the forces of sympathy and antipathy (*NH* 8.59).[2] We also hear of Anaxilaus, author "Natural Forces" and another treatise with the intriguing name of "Dippings."[3] References to these authors are joined by others to Ps-Manetho, author of "On Natural Forces" (second to first century BCE),[4] and Nigidus Filigus who wrote on grammar and theology as well as the natural sciences (first century BCE).[5] This entire literature is lost and rarely mentioned in modern scholarship. The ideas discussed in the treatises, however, had widespread influence.[6] Ancient investigations of "natural" forces helped individuals understand and put the forces to work.

Decades ago Nilsson struggled to find a way of characterizing these ancient usages of "natural" and relate them to the late antique cosmology. He wrote

> Human beings, the lower animals, plants, stones, metals, were all conceived of as the carriers of mysterious forces which had the power to cure sickness and suffering and to procure men riches, good luck, honor, and wonderful potencies. . . . The

very word "physical" in later times commonly meant an occult property or potency.

(1948: 105)

"Occult" leads us towards magic. Elsewhere in the same article, however, Nilsson likened the forces to modern notions of gravitation and chemical affinities (1948: 109). These comparisons set up connections to modern scientific thinking. Many of the sayings attributed to naturalists remind us of scientific discourse more than occult ideas, such as the statement preserved in the *Geoponica* that the "naturalists" say that beans harm the heart (*Geoponica* 2.35.3, p. 179).

Many of the writers on natural forces (Bolos, Democritus and Anaxilaus) are implicated in the rise of alchemy. Pliny mentions, for example, a treatise by Democritus called "Artificial Substances." This term appears in later alchemical texts where it seems to mean metals produced by technical arts.[7] We have no citations from Anaxilaus' treatise but the title "Dippings" refers to a process employed first in jewelry making and metallurgy and then in alchemy. Alchemy, which emerged in the first three centuries, presents a rich example of ancient imagining about unseen forces, an example which has confounded modern scholars.

The term alchemy is itself medieval;[8] in the first centuries CE the term Sacred or Divine Art was used instead.[9] Arts were found in many areas of social practice, such as rhetoric, medicine and architecture (Barton 1994: 7). They included both theoretical investigation and, most importantly, the practical application of the theories.

The "Sacred Art" emerged in the first centuries CE as religious thinkers borrowed the prestige and success of the technical arts, setting up their pursuits as parallel enterprises. They adapted state-of-the-art metal working techniques to their own goals, creating a new mode of practical instruction with far-reaching theoretical underpinnings. "Stealing" metalworking techniques was similar to modern attempts to prove that penicillin and other recent scientific discoveries are already encoded in the Bible, thereby rubbing off on the text some of the enormous prestige science currently enjoys.

While the early techniques were familiar from other social contexts, the focus of the Sacred Art was unique. It aimed at speeding up the inherent changes which the natural world (including humans) was thought to undergo. For alchemical practitioners, metals were not static since the cosmos itself was not static. Regardless of each metal's status in the natural world and its place in the hierarchy of the cosmos, every metal is on its way to becoming gold. The alchemist speeds up the process, making the change happen within a few hours instead of over generations.

The immediate goal of the complex alchemical procedures was to impart a series of color changes to the metals; blackening, whitening, yellowing and then the most obscure, violet-making. Each color signifies how inspirited a metal is by revealing the spirit (*pneuma*) of the metal; it indicates to the outside world the inner nature of the metal (Forbes 1964: 140). Changes in color are indications of the inner changes the metals undergo as they work their way up the ladder from the most earthly to the most heavenly.

The contributions of Maria the Jewess, which we will look at in some detail, are preserved for us by Zosimos (late third/early fourth century).[10] Maria is a remarkable figure, scarcely recognized in modern scholarship despite the past decades of trawling for neglected female figures.[11] The fragments of her writings are far more extensive than those of male writers who are presumed to have been historical figures, and they present a coherent set of concerns, as we will see below.[12]

The existence of early alchemical treatises attributed to a Jewish woman is so surprising it is worth pausing for a moment to consider why this is the case. Since so much of the diversity of Judaism in the first three centuries has been lost she seems like an anomaly. It is unusual to find references to Jewish women who worked in esoteric traditions and were called divine. If we depended on the history written by the rabbis, she would not exist. While we do find many titles associated with women in synagogue and tomb inscriptions, such as "head of the synagogue" and "mother of the synagogue" these titles do not point towards the Sacred Arts (Brooten 1982).

Why then do we even have any remembrance of her? One of the reasons is the trope in Zosimos that women know the secrets of metals, discussed in more detail below. This trope appears to have been more powerful than competing stereotypes about women. Texts associated with the Sacred Art contain a number of references to women; in addition to Maria we find Theosebia, Zosimos' "sister" in esoteric study, Cleopatra and Thesis the Virgin. The Sacred Art was sometimes in later texts called "opus mulierum/the work of women," not without some truth in the case of Maria (Forbes 1948: 24).

A second reason for the preservation of someone like Maria is that female figures appear to have been viewed as legitimate conveyors of special knowledge when there was a practical side to their endeavors.[13] For now it is enough to point out that the very fact that she worked with pots and pans and not in the realm of pure dialectical thought may have helped make a place for her in the late antique imagination.

Zosimos was an active practitioner and compiler of alchemical treatises who was originally from Panopolis, but according to later writers (Suda) lived in Alexandria.[14] Zosimos' most famous work is a series of 28 treatises dedicated to various divine figures, though he also wrote other treatises.[15] Zosimos in turn quoted from the writings of Maria, sometimes referring to a specific treatise such as "On Furnaces," but often citing her without giving a source. The numerous citations from Maria found in Zosimos offer a portrait of a practitioner with a distinct personality and intriguing set of concerns. Maria was the technician's technician, offering criticism and improvements on accepted modes of operation, many of which became standard practice for centuries after her. The high regard for her writings is seen in numerous other writers besides Zosimos; a later Arabic writer Al Habib stated "No philosopher has taught the truth in clearer form."[16]

Maria is presumed to have lived in Alexandria as Zosimos did, although there is no direct evidence at all. Her dates are subject to dispute, the evidence again being scanty.[17] Zosimos refers to her as an "ancient" while later alchemists thought she was the sister of Moses.[18] The only treatises prior to Maria we known of are those of Ps-Democritus, which are dated anywhere from the early second century BCE to the first century CE.[19] The rich arguments Maria engaged in demonstrate that she worked in a milieu with more developed techniques than Ps-Democritus, placing her after the compositions of these treatises. Some of the devices she adapted for the Sacred Art appear to have been developed in the first century CE, making it unlikely she wrote any earlier than the early second century CE. These include the distillation process in general and the glass still in particular (Keyser 1990: 362–3). In addition, her name is well represented in the list of Jewish women's names from the first centuries as compiled by Tal Ilan (1989).

Zosimos preserved numerous citations from her writings since Hebrews and Jews were cast as central figures in his history of the Sacred Art.[20]

> There are two sciences and two wisdoms: that of the Egyptians and that of the Hebrews, which latter is rendered sounder by

justice. The science and the wisdom of the best dominate both: they come from ancient centuries.

("The True book of Sophe the Egyptian and of the divine Lord of the Hebrews [and] of the powers of Sabaoth," Ber 3.4/2.1)

Sometimes Zosimos cited traditions which were borrowed from Jews without specifically attributing them to Jewish sources. His extensive discourse about the three-letter name Adam (אדם) "a name from the language of the angels" doubtless came from Hebrew exegetical traditions.[21]

Similarly, Olympiodorus, who wrote after Zosimos, stated

> It was the law of the Egyptians that nobody must divulge these things in writings. . . . The Jews alone have attained a knowledge of its practice, and also have described and exposed these things in a secret language. This is how we find that Theophilus son of Theogenes has spoken of all the topographic descriptions of the gold mines; the same is the case with the description of the furnaces by Maria and with the writings of other Jews.
>
> ("On the Sacred Art," Ber 2.4.35)

According to Zosimos' letter to Theosebeia, his "sister" in the Sacred Art, the ancient sacrifices of the Hebrews were prefigurations of the Sacred Art. He advised Theosebeia to copy the sacrifices which were recommended by Membres to Solomon, promising her that if she can copy them, operating in this manner she will obtain the proper, authentic, and natural tincture.[22]

More specifically, and most importantly in regards to Maria, Zosimos repeated the popular story that knowledge of metal-working came down from heaven by means of angels who revealed it to Jewish women.

> The ancient and divine books say that certain angels were taken by passion for women. They descended to earth and taught them all operations of nature. As a result, he [Zosimos] says, they fell and remained outside of heaven, because they taught men all that is wicked and of no profit to the soul. These Scriptures also say that from them the giants were born. Their initial transmission of the tradition about these arts came from Chemes. He called this book the Book of Chemes, whence the art is called "chemistry."
>
> (Syncellus, *Ecloga Chronographia* 23.9–24.12, Mosshammer)

It is impossible to know where Zosimos found this widely-circulating legend.[23] Since the Jews were not known for revealing their secret knowledge, turning to Jewish women was one way of gaining access to the traditions.[24]

Any texts attributed to Jewish women must have had a special resonance with him. Among these in turn Maria was his favorite; he calls her "divine."[25] Maria also saw her rituals as having a special connection to Jews. She warned, "Do not touch it with your hands. You are not of the nation (*genos*) of Abraham. You are not of our nation."[26] The notion of not touching is reminiscent of Biblical concerns about purity where touching could convey uncleanness. The restrictions give the procedures an aura of sacrality.

To locate Maria's specific contribution we must backtrack to the techniques used in metalworking and the alchemists prior to her. The first stage is "blackening" which created matter in its most embodied state, representing the very bottom of the scale of nature. At this stage the metal has no qualities except fusibility, which was the only quality necessary for moving the matter upward on the bodily scale towards greater liquidity.

The alloy was then subjected to the second stage, "whitening." This stage appears to be the same process used, for example, for silver making in the Ps-Democritan text (Forbes 1964: 14). The metal could be whitened by fusing tin or mercury to it, or by adding a small bit of silver called a "ferment." By these methods it was possible to "whiten" a mess of metal with only a small amount of "white." While this alloy would only be white on the outside, the fact that the inside was yellow would not have troubled an alchemist.[27]

The third stage was yellowing, again identical to the gold-making procedures of the earlier texts such as Ps-Democritus. Fusing could be done with gold ferment this time, or the metal was yellowed with "sulphur/divine water."[28] The sulphur water had to be produced before it could be employed and seems to have been made somehow from lead. The special water was used because "it produces the transformation; by its application you will bring out what is hidden inside; it is called 'the dissolution of bodies'"[29] The resulting yellow substance could then turn other substances yellow.

The final and most obscure stage is ιοσις: "purple-tincturing," perhaps making the amalgam purple or violet or perhaps simply cleaning it and taking away the rust (Hopkins 1934: 97–8; Taylor 1949: 49–50).[30] This step produced a "tincture of gold" which was believed to be the essence from which more gold could be produced. Zosimos explains, "It is the tincture forming in the interior [of the gold] which is the true tincture in violet, which has also been called the Ios of gold" ("The Four Bodies," Ber 3.19.3)."

Variations on these techniques appear in the main source for pre-Marian technique, the writings by Ps-Democritus. Similar techniques also appear in the earliest extant texts associated with alchemy, two papyri which appear on the surface as handbooks for metal-workers (Leiden X and Stockholm) but whose recipes do not look as if they will succeed.

When we turn to the excerpts from Maria preserved in Zosimos we find an explosion of technique accompanied by numerous new devices and instruments. Unlike Ps-Democritus, for example, her writings include the vocabulary of transmutation and the addition of techniques of distillation. Understanding Maria's citations involves mapping a plethora of objects: furnaces, lamps, water baths, dung-beds, reverberatory furnaces, scorifying pans, crucibles, dishes, beakers, jars, flasks, phials, pestles and mortars, filters, strainers, ladles, stirring rods, stills, and sublimatories (Taylor 1949: 46).

Maria's contributions are diverse; in the main she elaborates on and refines the pre-existing four-step procedure of changing the color of the metal.[31] She brags, for example, that her process for "blackening" is better than that used by others. Her copper and sulphur mixture is superior to the metal of magnesium since it is black all the way through and not just on the surface.[32]

Maria invented new devices to be used in these procedures. One device is even named after her, the "*balneum Mariae*" or water-bath, still used today for the slow heating of chemicals. The device is a form of double boiler. The substance to be heated is placed in an inner bowl, which is then placed in an outer container filled with water. It is unlikely that she invented this procedure (or all of the other procedures that are associated with her), but she may well have been the first to develop its use in the Sacred Art.[33]

Besides the water bath, we also find an ash bath (thermospodion). For example, Maria states "Take the sulphur water and a little of the adhesive, put it on the hot ash bath, for thus they say among themselves that the water is fixed" (Zosimos, "On the Sacred and Divine Art," Ber 3.11.1). Here again she is adapting a widely used device. The ash- or sand-bath, another of her devices, was well known from Greek and Roman doctors who used them to prepare their medicines and from the cookbooks of the period, for instance that of Apicus Coelius.

Maria is also closely associated with distillation devices, that is, with devices that collect some form of distillate into a receiving flask via a tube.[34] With distillation, the relationship between means and ends is altered from earlier techniques. Simply put, distillation can accomplish many ends but metalworking is not one of them. Sulfur, for example, which is frequently mentioned in this regard, cannot be distilled (Taylor 1949: 45).

It is significant that distillation was used only for treating and coloring metals and not for the more successful uses to which distillation can be put, such as making alcohol. Distillation was particularly suitable for Maria not because it worked but because the technique fitted her overall strategy of making solids into liquid. Producing steam was a model of the general transformation from earthly to heavenly she sought.

A variant on the still associated with Maria is the tribikos, which has three separate arms for collecting distillate.[35] Another device, a kerotakis, gets its name from the term for an artist's palette used for holding the pigment while painting.[36] The pigments (white, black, yellow and red) were mixed with wax on the kerotakis and were then ready for use. In the Sacred Art, the kerotakis was put inside a still, to hold the metals to be treated. The still was set up in such a way that the vapor rose in it, already in a modified state, and then fell upon the substance resting on the kerotakis. Since the still was made out of glass, it was possible to see the metallic substance inside change color as it reacted with the special vapor.[37]

The processes for which these devices were employed are described using a variety of Greek verbs, the particular nuances of which are sometimes hard to determine, but which all refer in some way to the distillation process. "Sublimation" (εκφνσαω) appears to have been a sub-part of the distillation process, with "sublimed" vapors being used to treat the metals by distillation. In a discussion on "metallic bodies" Maria complains about prior technique: "She wished to show that we do not sublimate well" (Ber 3.12.1). The sublimation process leads to a preliminary result of "shadowless" copper and gold. "'Sublimate vapors,' Maria says, 'until the sulphurous substance volatilizes (*θευγει*) with the shadow (which obscures the metal) and copper with no shadow will be produced'" ("On the Substances," Ber 3.12.7).[38] The point of being shadowless is that it is on its way to losing its bodily substance.

The basic change to which all of these procedures is directed is transforming the metal from the state of having a body to not having one. Maria states, "If the corporeal is not rendered incorporeal, and the incorporeal corporeal, nothing that one awaits will take place."[39]

If we have only a vague understanding of the processes she advocates, we have even less of a clear sense of what these procedures were performed on. Much to the chagrin of modern scholars, the Sacred Arts employed their own nomenclature for metals. Basic to the esoteric nature of these texts is a secret language of metals. Metals as we know them cannot affect other metals; only when they are treated do they become agents of change. The ideology of "ferments" points to the special properties of the metals employed; none of them were the same as their mundane counterparts. Everything has its own nomenclature.[40] "Our lead becomes black," Maria explains, "while common lead is black from the beginning."[41]

Maria's techniques are preserved without extensive theological introductions or commentaries. We do find some important ideas outlined in Ps-Democritus' only extant text, "Physical Things and Mysteries" (φυσικὰ καὶ μυστικά).[42] This text begins with formulas for dyeing cloth purple and then switches abruptly into a narrative about Democritus' search to learn how to "harmonize" nature. His search ends dramatically with the revelation of a phrase engraved on a pillar in a temple: "Nature rejoices in nature and nature conquers nature and nature masters nature." This cryptic saying implies that natural processes can be used to change nature, to overcome nature.

This is a very optimistic view; the means for getting beyond the natural world are available in the natural world. Based on this premise it is necessary to learn everything possible about the natural world since all answers are contained in it. If nature conquers nature, natural processes will ultimately lead to the cosmic changes sought by religious practitioners. This positive attitude to the natural world is striking and is crucial to the development of the Sacred Arts.

Zosimos also articulated a theology of alchemy, drawing analogies between transforming metals and redeeming humans. These analogies align the Sacred Art with tropes of the first man's fall into the body, of his resulting subjection to Fate, and of striving to transform nature and thereby ascend beyond the body to the immortal world of the spirit.[43] For Zosimos, becoming incorporeal is a means of overcoming Fate ("On the Letter Omega," section 7). But in his version these tropes do not become standard "dualistic" thinking with a starkly negative valuation of everything on earth and a positive valuation only on heavenly existence; instead they retain a more positive attitude towards the natural world since it is in fact changing and changeable.

From the ancient view these pursuits were driven by the same model of ancient divine wisdom which motivated so many of the rites discussed in the chapters above. Just as some of the rites in *The Book of Secrets* can be understood as modified sacrifices, the work over alchemical fires was also understood to be a derivation from ancient sacrificial practices. Unlike the rituals from the handbooks, these rites appear to have been completed in silence. This lack of verbal formulas is not as surprising as it might seem at first, since many ancient sacrificial practices appear to have been carried out in silence.

Modern attitudes towards these rites are highly ambivalent. Writers on natural forces have come to embody *both* magical and scientific thought in modern eyes. "Alchemy proper began," a recent article states, "when a neo-pythagorean [i.e., Bolos] applied magical notions of sympathy and antipathy to the Egyptian techniques."[44] Anaxilaus is labeled a magician in numerous modern studies, following Wellman's classic study (1928).[45] Exactly what kind of a threat or annoyance Anaxilaus posed to the authorities is unknown. It is assumed that he was expelled from Rome by Augustus in 28 BCE because he was a magician.

Yet, at the same time, investigations of "natural" forces represent from the modern viewpoint the origins of scientific thought. Alchemists employed metals in highly technical ways and so have an aura about them of being more scientific than many of the rituals we have examined so far. Much recent scholarship on alchemy is the product of historians of science for whom it represents early scientific thought.[46]

During the first three centuries explanations based on natural forces were explicitly excluded from notions of magic. Origen, for example, described the "natural" effects of Jesus' death. This "natural" explanation helps us begin to understand what is too complex for most people.

> For it is possible that there is in the nature of things, for certain mysterious reasons which are difficult to be understood by the multitude, such a virtue that one just man, dying a voluntary death for the common good, might be the means of removing wicked spirits, which are the cause of plagues.
>
> (*CC* 1.31)[47]

For Origen, other deaths, including those of martyrs and even Jephthah's daughter had the same "natural" effect. Knowledge of "natural antidotes and prophylactics" such as the instinctual use of fennel by serpents is also by definition not magic (*CC* 4.86).[48]

Christians may only learn after death "the reasons certain properties are associated with certain roots or herbs, and other herbs and roots, on the contrary repel [or avert]" (*DePr* 2.11.5).[49]

A Jewish-influenced prayer in "The Eighth Book of Moses" in the Greek papyri (*PGM* 13.154) states "Your natural name in Egyptian is Adlabiaeim."[50] Morton Smith translates the term "natural" as "magical," annotating it "with power to produce tangible effects."[51] A better translation than Nilsson's "occult potency" and Smith's "magical" might be "naturally powerful." This translation points to the mysterious and powerful forces in the world which effect its operations but which are obscure to the average person. The name "Adlabiaeim" seems to have special efficacy based on its natural relation to a supernatural power. So too, daimons respond "naturally" to their names according to Origen (*ExMar* 46).

Alchemical pursuits attempted to model natural processes, the slow natural changes which transform every part of the cosmos. The attitude towards the natural world reflected a synthesis of traditional locative themes, clinging to a positive evaluation of the natural world, but combined with a strong desire to reach utopian, otherworldly goals. As such, they sought to transform all of existence. Natural forces are not directly visible to the eye. Claims to employ these forces are likely to elicit the same skepticism as do claims to employ supernatural forces. The demarcations between natural and supernatural can also be confusing since, as we have seen, in ancient views, what we call supernatural forces work "naturally." Imposing modern notions of "magic" on these intricate ideas clarifies nothing; neither the gods nor nature work by magic. Perhaps the most important point is that we recognize the ancient attempts to demarcate a category of "natural" and to use it to explain the workings of the world, including divine forces. The greater one's knowledge of these forces, the more dramatic interventions could be. It was possible to imagine transforming the cosmos while working with a handful of the lowest earthly matter.

5
DIVINE POWER, HUMAN HANDS

Becoming gods in the first centuries

> Israel is called gods because it is written: I say, "You are gods."
> (*Tanhuma Qedoshim* 37.5 on Ps 82:6)

> The name of gods is given to them [Christians], for they will be enthroned along with the other gods who are set first in order under the Savior.
> (Clement, *Strom* 7.10)

An integral part of imagining magic is imagining the figure of the magician. Numerous figures were denounced as magicians in the first three centuries. Some are well known to us, such as Jesus, Apollonius of Tyana, and Apuleius; others are more obscure, such as Theudas known only from a single reference in Josephus (*Ant* 20.97).

One approach to investigating the figure of the magician would be to run through the points developed in Chapter 1 and tick off the reasons why someone might be labeled a magician. He (or she) might have harmed someone (even when trying to help), belong to a socially liminal group, or be presumed to operate via evil powers. These individuals were threats because of the amount of power that they were thought to wield.

The central question to be addressed in this chapter is not to retrace the contours of these charges but to ask the general question of how much access humans were thought to have to divine power. The power of the person charged as a magician seems anomalous to us unless we locate it within the context of the general sweep of power attributed to humans in the first three centuries. The mirror images of holy man and magician both depended on social conceptions of what kinds of supernatural power a human could employ, or be.

In the older visions, both Greek and Hebrew, the major barrier between humans and gods was that humans were destined for miserable existences in Hades or Sheol after their death.[1] In both Homer and the Hebrew Scriptures unhappy shades in the underworld lament their bleak existence. "Triumph over death is one achievement denied to humanity," Sophocles stated flatly (*Antig* 361).

With the rise of notions of the afterlife, this distinction was no longer so clear. Among the earliest notions of an afterlife to appear in Jewish texts was belief in astral immortality, that is, eternal life as a divine star (Cumont 1949). The book of Daniel predicts that "wise leaders shall shine like the bright vault of heaven, and those who have guided the people in the true path shall be like the stars forever and ever" (Daniel 12:3). Similar claims are found in Wisdom of Solomon 3:7 and in 1 Enoch 104:2.[2]

Post-death divinization as a star articulated with the idea that humans might be divine beings on earth. From a few early references, such as the claim that Empedocles was a god on earth (DK B115, B119 p. 356, 359), this idea became much more widespread. Morton Smith identified five individuals who were considered supernatural by their followers in the first century CE (1965: 743). These figures blurred the line between human and divine in a manner which would have been shocking in the older locative worldview.

In his succinct manner Nock stated, "to put on immortality was in Greek tantamount 'to become a theos/god'" (1951: 215). The equation of gaining immortality and deification was true in the minds of some Jews and Christians, as we will see below. Without either becoming THE deity or the focus of worship, humans could make the dramatic change from earthly to divine existence.

In the first centuries CE the notion of deification "was often expressed with a boldness which surprises moderns who have been brought up to think of the category of divinity as infinitely remote" (Nock 1951: 214). These claims go against modern stereotypes of Judaism and Christianity, or monotheism generally. The very idea of deification is thought, incorrectly, to smack of polytheism (Lattey 1916: 257).

In Jewish, Christian and Greco-Roman texts the transformation of a human into a divine being was thought to be effected by a stunning variety of techniques and combinations of techniques: burial, a vision of the deity, an ascent through the heavenly realm, being a vegetarian, and being drenched in blood, dipped in water, or drowned in the Nile.[3] In order to understand how these rituals emerged we will begin with the first hints of deification of humans in Jewish texts (first century BCE) and then consider the "routinization" of these techniques in the later centuries.

The emergence of deification techniques

Deification via ascent and hymn-singing in Jewish texts

Rich language about the transformation of humans into divine beings occurs in several places in the texts found in the Qumran library. These texts, composed just before and at the beginning of the time parameters of our study, include many images of the fusion of humans into the heavenly chorus and cult. The image of a heavenly liturgy goes back to Isaiah's report that the seraphim recite "Holy, holy, holy, is the Lord of Hosts, the whole earth is full of his glory" (6:3) and Ezekiel's mention of divine praise (1:3). The heavenly cult, richly developed from these few Biblical references, superseded the earthly one in endless Jewish texts from the Qumran scrolls to rabbinic texts.[4] The Qumran texts such as *Songs of the Sabbath Sacrifice (4QShirSabb)* detail the heavenly priesthoods along with other participants in the heavenly cult and the heavenly temple (based on Ex 25–31, 35–40).

The shift in location of the cult from earth to heaven confused many of the older locative categories. Humans and deity no longer met only in the earthly Temple. Now participation of any type in the cult involved ascending to the heavenly realm. The Qumran hymns describe a merging of selected humans into the heavenly chorus, giving the humans a new and much elevated status.[5] These human priests observe the angels of the divine presence, which means that they now function up in the heavens. The hymns do not claim that the humans surpass the highest angels who are still described as superior.[6] Nor does the text explicitly state that humans are now divine beings; the implications of merging with the angels is left unarticulated.[7] Later rabbinic texts will more explicitly place humans above angels.[8]

Qumran Scroll *Blessings* (*1QSbs*) offers a priestly blessing which explicitly merges humans and angels. The prayer exploits the priestly blessing in Numbers 6: 24–6, extending and redirecting it towards a new goal.

> May the Lord bless you . . . and set you as a splendid ornament
> in the midst of the Holy Ones . . .
>
> (3.25–6)

> May you be as an angel of the Presence in the holy Abode for the glory of God of hos[ts]. May you attend upon the service in the Temple of the kingdom and decree destiny with the angels of the Presence, [and may you be in] common council [with the holy ones] for eternal time and for all everlasting ages.
>
> (4.25–6)

While the Biblical blessing channeled the deity's blessing to an individual via a priest, ("May the Lord cause his face to shine upon you"), here the blessing transforms the priest himself. The priest is both the speaker and the object as the blessing cycle recycles the divine power of the blessing towards his own transformation. The power of the blessing and its efficacy still comes from the deity, but the manner in which it is channeled through the priest heightens the status of the priest himself. He is part of the heavenly class of beings who attend upon the divine cult.

Another Qumran collection of hymns, *Songs of the Sabbath Sacrifice* (*4QShirSabb*), is structured such that the singing of hymns traces the reciter's ascent from the earth through each ascending section of the heavenly court to its inner core.[9] The text contains intricate descriptions of the angelic cult in heaven; uttering each level of description marks the reciter as having arrived at that specific level of the heavens. Traversing each level is by definition an ascent, since the location of the cult is in heaven and the person sings the hymns is clearly now "there" as well. The implications of this ascent are not made explicit; that is, it is not clear whether the human has undergone some type of experience which has permanently changed him.[10]

Another scroll (*4QMa*), a variant reading of the *War Scroll*, describes an individual who becomes one of the "elim/gods" (M. Smith 1990). The phrase "I shall be reckoned with gods and established in the holy congregation" appears to describe a transformation of an earthly being into some type of divine being. This brag, as Smith pointed out, makes more sense coming from someone originally mortal than from an angel. The text gives us no hint of exactly how someone merits being counted among the gods.

All of these texts share the emphasis on ascent to the heavenly world found in numerous contemporary texts such as the Enoch literature. In the *Apocalypse of Abraham* (first to second centuries CE?), for example, Abraham recites a dense list of divine praises (Eternal one, might one, Holy El, God autocrat) taught to him by an angel and thus arrives in the seventh heaven (17:2–19; 19:4–6).

The Qumran texts, however, locate ascent not as a literary theme connected to long-dead figures, but imagine an active participation in the life of the heavenly realm as available to at least some individuals.

Very near in time to the composition of the later Scrolls from Qumran, Philo also described the role of hymn-singing in ascent. Scriptures do not say where Moses was buried so Philo imagined that Moses did not die but instead was "translated" from the earthly sphere to the heavens. At his death Moses rose through the sky singing hymns and leading the other cosmic elements in song (*Vita* 76–9).

If only this text survived we would lack any clear idea of what happened to Moses, just as we must guess about the transformation of those who sing the Qumran hymns. Other texts of Philo, however, describe Moses' divinization much more clearly. Scriptures state that the deity made Moses "as a god before Pharaoh"; Philo read this line as a literal statement about deification. Moses' prophetic mind "becomes divinely inspired and filled with God," evidence that "such men become kin to God and truly divine" (*QuesEx* 29; cf. *SacAbel* 9). The holy soul is divinized[11] by ascending through the heavens beyond the world to where there is "no place but God" (*QuesEx* 40).

Since the matriarchs and Moses' wife, according to Philo, had supernatural conceptions based on divine paternity, their children (and thus the children of Israel) were semi-divine to begin with. Ascent in this case is a return to an original home base. Imagining that humans can become divine is intimately connected with the notion that some humans are not simply human to begin with.

In all these texts we see the pressure from the utopian cosmology to make the higher realm accessible to humans. At the same time some humans may turn out to have been divine beings in human disguise, for whom death was not a barrier.

Roman deification by burial and cremation

Worship at tombs was an ancient practice in both Roman and Greek cultures (M. Smith 1983: 96ff.). Plutarch reminded his readers that the Romans honored the tombs of their fathers "even as they do the shrines of the gods, they declare that the dead person has become a god at the moment when first they find a bone" (*RomanQues* 14). These practices flourished in the first three centuries CE. Epitaphs, often hard to date, but known to be from the period of the empire, evince a rich variety of notions about post-burial deification.[12] Clement of Alexandria derided his non-Christian neighbors for the number of tombs they worshipped (*Protrep* 3).

A special form of immortalization was reserved for children who died young, a practice commented on in Jewish and Christian texts.[13] Wisdom of Solomon 14:15 mocks the grief of a father for his dead son whom he "now honored as a god what was once a human corpse." Despite ironic, even hostile, portrayals in these sources, similar reassurances that their children were living happily as immortal figures in heaven also circulated in Jewish and Christian circles. While some thought that the untimely dead, including children, were destined to roam the earth as trouble-causing daimons, others were sure that children were more likely than most to ascend to the highest reaches and live among the gods.

In the late first century BCE, the Romans were debating the divinization of Julius Caesar (Price 1987).[14] These debates and the rituals of deification that evolved in the next century, point to the growing acceptance of the notion that a human (or at least an emperor) could become a god even while alive. Not only was the person deified, but the individual was also worshiped, that is, expected to intervene on behalf of supplicants.[15]

The question of whether Julius Caesar was considered a god in his lifetime is a source of modern debate, just as it was during his lifetime (North 1975). One of the few extant contemporary witnesses, Cicero, clearly felt that Caesar received honors inappropriate for a human. These honors included putting a statue of Caesar in the Quirinus temple and carrying a statue of him along with one of Romulus-Quirinus in the festival procession.[16] After his death Caesar was awarded "couch, image, pediment, priest," that is, all the accoutrements of a divine cult.[17] While Cicero found these moves offensive in relation to Julius Caesar, he was willing to conceive of a human (Pompey) as an angel sent down to humanity from the gods, much like Philo's Moses.[18] He used the term ἀπόθέωσις: "deification" in his attempt to honor his daughter after her death. Cicero ordered a shrine built for her and not a tomb, hoping to "get as close to deification as possible."[19] His desire for divine honors for his daughter carried none of the political implications that divine honors for Caesar did, but it required a similar view of human possibility.

The funeral rituals of the Roman emperors were a particularly dramatic publicizing of the deification of humans via cremation. The three main descriptions of the deification-by-ascent rituals for Roman emperors, two by Dio Cassius[20] and one by Herodian,[21] share many elements. The rituals were modeled closely after the funeral rites of Roman nobility at the end of the Republic. Just as in a noble funeral, an effigy of the body was displayed in the Forum to a crowd of mourners who wore special dress. After a funeral procession, which included the display of masks of the ancestors, the dead person was eulogized in an oration and the body taken from the Forum and cremated. The scope and drama of the funeral of an emperor was magnified greatly from the model of the funerals of nobles. Augustus was a new type of *pater patriae* with a larger "family." A greater range of ancestral masks was carried in the funeral procession and a Senate decree in effect treated all women as daughters or wives of the emperor (Price 1987: 63–5). A new element, the release of an eagle from the tower where the effigy was burned, functioned as a concrete mapping or model of the transfer of the emperor's spirit to the world of the gods.

The divine cult apparatus was added in the form of divine honors awarded to the dead emperor. These included priests and sacrifices, as Price calls it, "the apparatus of divine cults" (1987: 58). These honors, plus others, such as the absence of prayers offered on the day in remembrance of the dead, made the worship of the emperor similar to that of a deity and not a dead ancestor. The classic narratives of Romulus' and Hercules' deification by means of a funeral pyre were enacted in the burning of the emperors' earthly bodies. The body needed to be destroyed since the common trope held that bodies couldn't ascend. Cicero, for example, stated that the bodies of Hercules and Romulus did not ascend since what is earth cannot leave earth (*DeRep* III.40).

The burning of the wax effigy meant that there were no "human" remains after the ritual whatsoever, and not even the bones left after a cremation. This marked the sharp distinction between divinization, which was not related to tombs or bodily remains, and the more common worship carried out at the tombs of close relatives or heroes and dependent on having at least one piece of the body. Athenaeus preserved a fragment of Aristotle where he explained that "If my purpose had been to sacrifice to Hermeias as a god, I should never have built for him the monument as for a mortal, nor, if I had wished to make him into the nature of a god, should I have honored his body with funeral rites" (*Deip* 15.697a).[22] In the case of divinization, the sequence of a funeral pyre followed by an eagle release marks the stages of the ritual: the total destruction of the body (or effigy) followed by a sign that the divine part is now in the heavenly realm.

Dio Cassius (45.7) uses the tantalizing term ἀπαθανατίζω: "deify" to refer to this process.[23] In its earlier usages this term was associated with exotic foreign groups who were thought to know the secrets of immortality, especially the Thracians and their leader Zalmoxis.[24] A healing song is traced to some of Zalmoxis' physicians, "who knew how to make someone immortal."[25] Herodotus reports the claim of the Getea, that they do not die, but go instead to Zalmoxis (*Hist* 4.94). These people are referred to simply as "the deifiers."[26] We find no hints in the early Greek texts as to how the Getea became immortal. Such "deifiers" were thought primarily to reside far from the center of Greek culture, though some sects within the culture, such as the Pythagoreans, may have been referred to by the same term (Linforth 1918: 27–8).

Strabo used the term in his description of an incident where an Indian, whom we are told was wearing only a loincloth, came bearing gifts to Caesar. He threw himself onto a burning pyre in order to "immortalize" himself. The inscription marking this event reads: "Here lies Zarmanochegas, an Indian from Bargosa, who immortalized himself in accordance with the ancestral customs of Indians" (*Geo* 15.1.73). Dio Cassius talks about the same incident, which clearly impressed the Romans, wondering whether the Indian threw himself into the fire alive in order to make a display to Augustus or because it was a tradition in his culture (54.9). With Dio Cassius the term is specifically associated with the transforming funeral pyre of the emperor cult; thus with the cult of the emperor the term "immortalize" moves from Thrace to Rome, from an exotic philosophical minority or the act of a near-madman to the literal center of town. Josephus' claim that the Essenes "immortalize" the soul is evidence that such claims could reasonably be made about a Jewish philosophical minority and were even likely to bring them a certain prestige (*Ant* 18:16–8).

As exaggerated as the divine honors given to Julius Caesar may have seemed to Cicero, Augustus' funeral points to a routinization of these ideas in the first century. It signifies the general acceptance that burning funeral pyre plus ascent was a mode of divinization. This model presented the emperor as a mediating figure between human and divine, setting up the emperor and his family as semi-human/semi-divine beings.[27] It is hard to imagine that such a concrete, and in many ways simple, model of deification did not reinforce the possibility that others could attain the same fate. The slippery slope leads first to the deification of relatives[28] and lovers of the emperor. The most famous case was Hadrian's lover Antinous, who drowned in 130.[29] Since drowning in the Nile was thought to be a form of deification, his claim to divine status was doubly reinforced.[30] Numerous coins and statues of Antinous dressed as Apollo and other divine figures are evidence of the widespread cult dedicated to him.[31] The Senate itself became official "deifiers" since the deification had to be ratified by one of its members.[32] The self-immolation of some of Otho's soldiers on his funeral pyre may have been an attempt to extend the deification process to witnesses of the ritual.

In the Roman evidence no single pattern of divinization emerged, even among the emperors and their families. Some individuals were deified only outside of Rome, as in the cult of Antinous. Others were depicted as gods only on more small-scale private commemorations such as a gem. A small cameo, for example, depicts the apotheosis of Germanicus, adopted son of Tiberius. Germanicus sits on the gem on an eagle as Victory crowns him with a wreath (Richter 1968: 120).

The rich imagery of deification-through-burial articulates with the development of pseudo-burials, though many of the references to these rituals are hard to date precisely.[33] Paul describes baptism as a means of participating in Christ's death, burial and resurrection (Rom 6:3–4). Apuleius tells of a symbolic death and rebirth in his *Metamorphosis* where he is buried and then raised to a new life (Book 11).[34] According to a very complex description in Proclus, one ritual involved burying a participant up to his neck, since his head was the only part of him which was already immortal (*ThPl* 4.9 p.30 l.17). The rest of the body would be made immortal by this pseudo-burial.

A deification ritual found in the Greek papyri exploits the same model of a pseudo-burial (*PGM* 4.153–285). Here the text instructs the practitioner to lie down naked under a sheet wrapped "like a corpse" (4.176). He then recites a series of "I am he" formulas, identifying himself as a companion of the god. The appearance of a sea hawk who strikes the man with his wing is a sign that the participant can claim to the god that he has "been united with your holy form." As a result he returns with a "godlike nature" (4.220).

Deification techniques in early Christian texts

The rise of early Christianity offers new kinds of evidence about deified humans, including theological texts which spell out the concepts more clearly than any Roman writings did. Early Christian texts evince a wide variety of stances on the basic idea that the deity became a man in order that people could in turn become divine. Language of commonality with divinity appears, for example, in the New Testament (2 Pet 1:4).[35] The vague language of the New Testament does not tell us anything about how one becomes divine. Other texts point us to specific aspects of the life of a Christian which enable the transformation; some of these are general modes of life and some are specific rituals.

General language of deification for those who live a good Christian life runs through many early Christian texts. For Justin, the Word "by his instruction makes mortals immortal, makes men gods" (*Orat* 5) and "only those who live near to God in holiness and virtue are immortalized (ἀπαθανατίζεσθαι)" (*1Apol* 21). Theophilus of Antioch explicitly argued that it is possible to gain the reward of immortality by keeping the commandments and thereby becoming a god (*Autolyc* 2.27).

The possibility that humans could become gods, or equal to the angels (ἰσάγγελος), was particularly important to Clement of Alexandria (*Strom* 7.10, cf. Butterworth 1916). Humans are all created in the image of the divine in that they possess a mind which is already divine. They must learn to cast off the ways of the body and through their discipleship to Christ, learn to live a life without any human passions. They can, therefore, "practice here on earth the heavenly way of life by which we are deified (ἐκθεούμεθα)" (*Paed* 1.12). Hearing the scriptures and attending to the truth it is "as if a god is produced out of a man" (*Strom* 7.16). The human soul "practices to be a god (μελετᾷ εἶναι θεός)" (*Strom* 6.14).

Clement cited Psalm 82:6 – "I say: You are gods" – more than once as proof of the deification of Christians. In the *Stromates* he interpreted the verse as meaning that humans will become gods if they throw off the passions of the body as much as possible (*Strom* 2.20). Elsewhere the same verse is used as proof of a complex procedure from baptism to enlightenment then to adoption into the divine family, perfection and finally deification (ἀπαθανατίζω) (*Paed* 1.6).[36]

In addition to leading the right kind of life, knowledge can also deify, since heavenly teachings bestow the boon of making a man into god (θεοποιῶν) (*Protrep* 11). Clement reminded his readers that Socrates called a dialectician a god. Thus everyone who contemplates Platonic Ideas lives "as a god among men" (*Strom* 4.15).

Many of Clement's statements have implications for understanding Christian rituals since they become the vehicles for deification. The transformative role of baptism, for example, is familiar from

Paul (Rom 6:3–4) and thus from Jewish circles. Gaining immortality by means of a dip in a font of water is mentioned, for example, in an inscription from the first century CE from the Ino-leukothea cult in Asia Minor. Farnell, who wrote on this cult, argued that a reference to resurrection in the Minyah legend of Ino-leukothea developed into a ritual of rebirth (1916). The myth was acted out in a ritual dip in a fountain which functioned as means of deification (ἀποθεωθεὶς ἐν τῷ λέβητι: "divinizing in the fountain").

Ascent techniques routinized

The technique of singing hymns to ascend through the heavens and thereby be deified reappears in a variety of later ritual texts (third century and beyond). The use of hymns may have been so popular because it reflected both Scriptural models and the Greco-Roman trope common since Plato that songs (*epodai/carmina*) have tremendous power.[37]

In the middle of the second century, a father–son team of Juliani presented themselves as specialists in practices which lead to deification. The fragmentary *Chaldaean Oracles* associated with the father–son team claim that the person who engages in the special practices will be part of the angelic order (Fr. 137,138). The *Oracles* include tantalizing references to initiations, purifications and consecrations. While it is probably a mistake to reconstruct a single "Chaldaean" ritual from the surviving fragments of the *Oracles*, at least one of them appears to have been a ritual of ascent (ἄνοδος) where the soul leaves the body and returns to its heavenly abode, there gaining immortality.[38] With the help of angels, a worshipper is able to separate his soul from his body by a process of breathing techniques (inhaling the sun's rays).[39]

The *Mithras Liturgy*, found in an early fourth century Greek papyrus,[40] follows a soul on a complex journey past the planets and cosmic forces up to the highest heaven based on the recitation of complex hymns. The *Liturgy* states clearly that the process confers immortality; it includes an opening phrase ". . . for an only child, I request immortality" (476), an invocation to "give me over to immortal birth" (501), and a hailing formula which declares that the reciter has become immortal (647).

The ascent begins with a hymn combining letter sounds with creation imagery: "First origin of my origin, AEEIOYO, first beginning of my beginning, PPP SSS PHR[E]" (487ff.). Recitation of letter-strings equated with cosmic elements incorporates their transformative power into the prayers, much as angel names incorporated their power into the rites in *The Book of Secrets* ("and the sacred spirit may breath in me, NECHTHEN APOTOY NECHTHIN ARPI ETH" (510)). The individual is then instructed to

> Draw in breath from the rays, drawing up three times as much as you can, and you will see yourself being lifted up and ascending to the height, so that you seem to be in mid-air.
> (539–40)

These breathing techniques, including the making of hissing and popping sounds, enable the ascender to take off and begin his travel through the cosmos.[41] He is able to see "himself" as he separates off into two parts.

Once traveling towards the upper regions, the ascender tries to pass himself off as a star, that is, as a natural inhabitant of the heavens (570–5). The process depends in part on identification, with the individual literally re-defining himself as a cosmic being by reciting "I am a star" (574). Here beliefs about astral immortality, now centuries old, are illustrated by the actual transformations. As a ritual for immortalization, the *Liturgy* was probably originally meant to effect such a one-time transformation. The ritual has been re-edited and the outermost frame now relates the ritual to divination.[42]

The strategies used in the famous ascent[43] attributed to Rabbi Nehunya in *Hekhalot Rabbati* (fourth to sixth century) emerged as yet another variation on the theme of effective hymns.[44] This text is part of the collection of esoteric texts referred to as *hekhalot* (palace) or *merkabah* (chariot) texts which describe the heavenly cult with the fiery angelic choruses and, the summoning to earth of various angelic figures and transformation of humans into angels.[45] In this case the hymns include direct citations of heavenly liturgy, numerous divine names, and strings of letters from divine names.[46] The primary "fuel" of the trip is still "talk"[47] as seen in the ascent in the *Songs of the Sabbath Sacrifice*, but here the talk includes two additional levels of efficacy.[48] First, the hymns contain the exact same words that the heavenly chorus recites. This mode of direct citation fuses the human into the angelic unit more directly than in the *Songs*. What the priests in the *Songs* watched and reported on the heavenly chorus, the person who recites these hymns *does*. Second, the use of the letters and sounds of the divine names incorporates divine power into the hymns.[49]

The goal of the ascent in *Hekhalot Rabbati* is a slippery question.[50] Among hekhalot texts, promise of immortality is found most clearly in *Merkabah Rabbah*, which claims that it "will lengthen days to eternal life." Whatever its original goal, the ascent in *Hekhalot Rabbati* has been re-edited into a new frame, exactly as the *Liturgy* has, which promises that the ascent hymns will enable the practitioner to "see the deeds of men" and know what the future holds. Since divination is a less shocking goal than gaining immortality, the re-editing of the ritual into the divination frames is a sort of domestication.

In these ascent texts the dramatic elevation to heaven in the *Songs* has become routinized; Rabbi Nehunya says that knowing the ritual is like having a ladder in one's home. He easily negotiates between the earthly and heavenly spheres, leaving his body on earth while he traverses the heavens. While he is not called one of the "elim" he is an immortal being (son of the world to come) who straddles the earthly and heavenly worlds. So too Proclus, according to his biographer, ascended to the heavens at the age of 42 and found them resounding with immortality (Marinus, *VitaPro* 28).

In addition to the general use of hymns in ascent, we find tantalizing references to the use of the Kedusha formula from Isaiah 6:3 in deification rituals. The Cherubim recite this phrase when they carry the divine throne, and thus the phrase was already associated with being raised heavenwards in the Scriptural text.[51] The three-fold recitation of the term "holy" placed in the mouth of the heavenly beings was considered the essence of heavenly liturgy.

Jewish texts composed in Greek connect the recitation of the formula and divinization. The Christian *Apostolic Constitutions*, for example, includes liturgy long recognized to be of Jewish origin (Bousset 1979).[52] This early Christian liturgy preserves a Greek version of the Kedusha which predates much of the extant Hebrew liturgy. Having the text extant in Greek makes it easier to trace the echoes of the Kedusha in other Greek texts.

Sections of this text parallel hymns recited in another Greek ascent text, "Poimandres", the first text in the *Corpus Hermeticum* (Pearson 1981). The treatise is named after the revealing deity who speaks in the text (Poimandres) and who is identified with the thrice-great Hermes of Greco-Egyptian fame. By means of question and answer the revealing god teaches the initiate the basics of cosmology, the fall of man into bodily existence, and the final ascent back to God.

The Jewish elements in "Poimandres," including references to Genesis 1–2, have long been noted.[53] The connection between the hymnic ascent and the deification is made explicit in several places in the text, such as "This is the final good for those who have received the knowledge: to be made god" (Poim 26). At the end of the Poimandres text, as the figure ascends from earth to heaven and immortal life, he recites hymns which closely parallel the Kedusha in the *Apostolic Constitutions* (Poim 31; *AposCon.* 7.34–5).[54] It is exactly the recitation of the "holy" formulas which signal his final deification.

These Greek parallels help us interpret several cryptic rabbinic texts. Tanhuma, for example, hints but does not explain that Israel is called God, in the reference in Psalms "you are gods" because of the Kedusha.[55] This reference makes sense to us as a highly condensed reference to deification, much as it appeared in Clement of Alexandria. A strikingly similar idea about name change connected to deification also appears, again in condensed form, in rabbinic literature. Genesis 33:20, where Jacob builds an altar and calls it "El-elohe-Israel" is interpreted as meaning that Jacob was called "El", that is a god, by the deity (bMeg 18a). A similar theme appears in the midrash where Jacob claims that just as the Lord is the lord over all heavenly things, he is the lord over all earthly beings (*GenRab* 79.8).[56]

Philo's striking claims about Moses, that he was a divine being in human form, became more widespread not only in Christianity but in Jewish texts as well. A fragment of the Jewish text "Prayer of Joseph," preserved for us by Origen, revealed that Jacob was really an angel of high rank who was sent down to earth (J. Z. Smith 1978b: 24–66). So, too, a Jewish prayer in the *PGM* asks "Fill me with wisdom, empower me, Master . . . because I am an angel on earth, because I have become immortal" (7.7).

At the same time, by the end of the first three centuries Philo's technique of closing off the senses to permit the human mind to reconnect with its divine source became a cliché in later philosophical texts (*Mig*). Language of deification via dialectics is woven through the various tractates of the *Corpus Hermeticum*. The eleventh tractate argues that the path to deification is to realize that the entire cosmos is within oneself (*CH* 11.20).[57] The fourth tractate "A Discourse of Hermes to Tat" simply states that humans must choose to hate their bodies so that they can love their mind, which is part of the divine realm. Choosing to be engaged in the divine realm rather than the mortal one makes a human into a god (*CH* 4.7). Tractate 13 uses the language of being "born again" (*CH* 13.1, 3, 10 and *passim*), instructing the student to "leave the senses of the body idle and the birth of divinity will begin" (*CH* 13.7).[58]

All of these rituals and the ideas they reflect were contested in the first three centuries. Christians who were engaged in power struggles rejected claims to divinity made by their opponents. Thus Irenaeus railed against Christians who claimed special knowledge and considered themselves equal with the gods (*AdHaer* 4.38). Some rabbinic authorities argued so distinctly against the notion that people can become divine it disguises the fact that some individuals within their own communities believed in this idea.[59]

Despite opposition, ideas about deifying humans even before death continued to circulate in later centuries. Clement's claims were repeated by later Christian writers, including Hippolytus.[60] The role of the Eucharist in deifying the participant is clearly spelled out in Ps-Dionysius. Scriptural references to humans as the image of God (Gen 1:27ff. and 9:6) are discussed in rabbinic texts in terms reminiscent of the statues of rulers found throughout the Roman Empire. These statues were understood to be the closest copy to divinity on earth, and thus were used by the rabbis to reinforce the similarities between humans and the deity (M. Smith 1958: 478–9). Men have the same form of divinity, all the way down to the mark of circumcision, and they share his name and thus his glory (bBabaB 75b). Rabbinic literature also contains several dramatic statements about the human use of power that articulate closely with the elevated status of humans resulting from deification rites. Moshe Idel has drawn our attention to the rabbinic texts where individuals are able to either increase or decrease the Godhead. The midrashic interpretation of "through God we shall act with power" (Ps 60:14) is "In God we shall make power."[61] Such statements show rabbinic thinking on its way towards the later Kabbalistic Jewish doctrine of "making God" discussed by Idel (1988: 188–9).

Being born again, a second time, in a birth which makes one a son of God or of the world to come, remains a crucial part of later Christian and Jewish beliefs. The first birth is from a woman, and thus ensures nothing. The second birth, initiated by a priest or a rabbi, is the birth to eternal life. The range of deification rituals was astounding. The act of lying down or being buried and imitating death is equivalent to the statements in the *Liturgy* where the practitioner's body is being remade and to the discourse about being born-again in *Corpus Hermeticum*. In the first three centuries these ideas were not interpreted as vague metaphors, but as goals the appropriate rites could effect.

In *The Book of Secrets* joining the heavenly chorus co-exists with all sorts of other rites, located literally on top of them in the seventh heaven. So too in the *Greek Magical Papyri* rituals for gaining immortality are edited together with numerous other concerns. Becoming a heavenly being is not qualitatively different from other concerns, so the texts impute. In the first centuries, using human hands to employ divine power was always to some extent putting on the image of the deity. In some cases the rites effected not only the world around the practitioner, but the human hands themselves were completely transformed.

6
"EVEN THE DECENT WOMEN PRACTICE WITCHCRAFT"
Magic and gender in late antiquity

No matter where we look in the history of accusations of magic and witchcraft, women are over-represented. From denunciations of Biblical witches to modern Halloween cartoons, women take center stage. Since the imaginings about magic most often come from men, it is no surprise that women are so consistently the targets. It is tempting to see in these charges classic Freudian projections by men of all that they fear onto women. In those cases where we do find more men charged than women, we also find the particular social circumstances that made men, at least temporarily, more than women, the target of social hostilities.[1] Women are so often the targets of these attacks that we wonder for a moment whether this is one of those cross-cultural truths in which anthropologists delight.

Lest we leave this topic at the level of simple stereotypes we will examine one set of accusations made against women in the first three centuries CE. Our test-case is rabbinic literature, which, while it was redacted over several centuries (third to seventh centuries CE), contains many ideas which come from the first three centuries. These texts offer us such grandiose rhetoric about "women who engage in witchcraft" that it takes the breath away.[2] While men are theoretically as capable of indulging in magic as women, the gender skewing in accusations and rhetoric is striking. In an exegesis stunning in comparison to any remark about women and magic found in an oral culture, the Biblical verse "You shall not permit a witch to live (Ex 22:18)" is said to refer to a female figure since "mostly women are engaged in witchcraft" (bSanh 67a).

This attitude runs all the way from the Mishnah, the core document of rabbinic literature edited mid-third century to much later rabbinic texts. Witches appear and re-appear in numerous texts from the Mishnah's concern that increase in the number of wives is a cause of increased witchcraft (Hillel mAvot 2.7) to the statement attributed to Simon b. Yohai that "even the decent women practice witchcraft" (jKid 4.11). Women represent a constant set of worries throughout their lifecycle; fathers must worry that their young daughters will be seduced and that old women will engage in magic (bSanh 100b). Between these stages women were likely to be suspected of poisoning their husbands, or attracting them in the first place via strange potions.[3] It is dangerous to use discarded foodstuffs found by the road, since the daughters of Israel engage in sorcery (bErub 64b). Crossroads are an inherently suspicious place where supernatural spirits are likely to lurk. Given this, two women seen together at a crossroads were deemed likely to be engaging in witchcraft (bPes 111a). The fact that these women are in a public space and not a domestic one makes them suspicious.

This assemblage of quotations is somewhat distorting. Collecting quotes from the vast corpus of rabbinic texts edited over several centuries does not convey the whole picture about attitudes towards women. The rabbinic anecdotes speak with many voices and viewpoints on any topic, including women. The range of rabbinic opinions about and attitudes towards women is a subject of intense current debate. The point here is not to see the extent to which rabbinic texts prefigure modern feminist concerns. Interested readers can, for example, contrast Daniel Boyarin's claim that rabbinic recognition of female sexual desire reflects a more positive conceptualization of women then expected (1993) with Tal Ilan's comment that positive attitudes towards sexuality should not be equated with positive attitudes towards women (1996: 14). We should also not expect ancient sensibilities to match ours, since they will not, as Peter Brown has pointed out in his studies of ancient attitudes towards to the body (Brown 1998: 30). The limited task here is to look more closely at how at how statements about witchcraft and women come to warrant the intense interest they do and the dramatic – one is tempted to say paranoid – statements.

We have already seen that the Hebrew Scriptures closely associated women with magic and witchcraft. The prime model for witchcraft is the female practitioner in Exodus 22:18.[4] In other instances the charge of witchcraft is combined with charges of prostitution and illicit sexuality, reinforcing the suspicion of magic with the general fear of female sexuality. Prophetic texts associate harlotry and magical charms (Nah 3:4) while historical texts denounce women as harlots who engage in sorcery (Jezebel in 2 Kings 9:22).

Women were especially vulnerable since they did not hold any power in the Biblical religious institutions, such as the priestly circles. The editors of the Biblical text claimed that foreign women perverted Israelites' religious traditions, making women a general threat. To make matters worse, women had roles in ancient rituals which came under attack in the Bible. Ezekiel 13:17–23 presents an extensive prophetic diatribe against ancient practices related to the dead where women would "hunt for souls" while wearing wristbands and veils. Shifting attitudes to the dead led to the condemnation of these practices as magic, with the presence of female practitioners, once accepted but now suspect, reinforcing that view in later generations.[5]

The most famous "witch" incident, and the only one in the Hebrew Scriptures of any length which describes a female practitioner at work, is the story of Saul's request of the woman at Endor to summon Samuel from the grave (1 Sam 28). This story is a late addition by a Deuteronomic editor, projecting the ritual event back onto the early kingship period (Schmidt 1995). The story finds its closest parallels not in Canaanite practice at the time of Saul, but in later Mesopotamian necromantic rituals (seventh century BCE). In these rituals a ghost is questioned about the future for the purpose of "predicting the outcome of war as well as the destiny of a royal house" (Schmidt 1995: 118), exactly as is the case in the story about Saul.

The Deuteronomic editor projected the later necromantic rituals back onto Saul. All of this was done in order to cast aspersions on the early king and to answer the question: What could he have done that was so bad that kingship was taken away from him? Brian Schmidt explains, "In the final analysis, for the deuteronomic tradition, necromancy – more than any other rite – epitomizes the abomination of the Canaanite in the history of Israelite kingship." And the coup de grâce is that Saul consulted none other than a woman. The gendering of the event makes it that much more shocking and degrading for Saul.

Greco-Roman culture also had its stereotypes of witches. While the picture of the "magi" stemmed from the Persian priest,[6] an even more negative picture of female practitioners emerged in the same period (Gordon 1987: 80). Unlike the magi, the female figures had no redeeming features. While magi were thought to have access to ancient wisdom and a certain prestige, women are presented as isolated figures who threaten both family members (and potential mates) and the general social fabric. These women, who deal in the realms of healings (root-collectors) and family disputes (love, revenge), could not even claim to be part of ancient or complex technical traditions. They worked within the realm of their family or mercenarily for strangers on a "freelance" basis. References to them are excluded from any scholarly investigations such as Theophrastus' *On Plants* and its discussion of famous male root-cutters.

While both men and women used supernatural forces to gain lovers, the literary portrayals of women's actions are more likely to specifically associate these actions with magic, witchcraft, human sacrifice, rampant sexuality and other antisocial colorings. Theocritus' *Second Idyll* describes at length a hostile and vindictive woman who uses love incantations to lure back a wayward boyfriend, threatening that she will kill him if it does not work. No doubt women did engage in love rites, as did men. Love-rites as discussed in Chapter 3 were used for both wayward and uninterested spouses, as well as attracting new lovers. The difference is the particularly negative portrayal of women. Theocritus' unhappy woman is planning to murder her boyfriend. We look in vain for parallel and equally hostile portrayals of men engaged in this action, though we know from the physical ritual remains that figures bound in love recipes were often women.

Medea, while not directly called a witch in the early texts, is involved in all sorts of antisocial and destructive actions which make it clear that women with supernatural powers are active threats to everyone in their sphere. She effected her goals by illicit and suspect means, but she is presented in such a way as to make her path seem to be the natural one of women.[7] She is a full-blown fantasy of femininity gone wrong. Hostile, vindictive and dangerous, she kills her brother, poisons members of the royal family, and murders her own children.[8]

In general in Greek literature, Richard Gordon concludes, women are depicted as a curse and essentially false. Summing up the hostile imaginings associated with women he writes "Medea is an exaggerated version of this representation of women, dominated by nature, false, scheming and dangerous: and magic is part of the armory which gives this sex its power" (1987: 83).

Some of the most lurid prose in Greco-Roman literature is about the women who, as in the story of Saul, are associated with raising the dead. These unpleasant, often old and ugly, women live among or consort with the dead and in general pervert all the standards of civic society. Lucan's portrayal of the Thessalian witch Erictho is both vivid and repulsive (*BelCiv* 6).[9] Finding a corpse she "eagerly vents her rage on all the limbs, thrusting her fingers in the eyes, scooping out gleefully the stiffened eyeballs, and gnawing the yellow nails on the withered hand" (6.540–3). Lucan cast scorn on Pompey's son for visiting this witch, much as the Biblical editor attacked Saul. The more loathsome she is the more loathsome his request of her.

A variety of "human products" were no doubt used in numerous healing rituals. Pliny describes potential uses of saliva, urine, hair, sweat, the very first menstrual blood, first teeth which have fallen out, the blood of gladiators, bones from the hands of criminals, the tooth of a man killed by violence, the skull of a hanged man, and women's milk (*NH* 28). Some people believed in the efficacy of these items, and some other people no doubt tried to find and sell them. At the same time, all the doubts and discomfort as to whether these items were both effective and fitting for human use, some expressed by Pliny, were projected onto women. The resulting depictions of women collecting and using body parts are truly disgusting, filled with corpses, bodily fluids and ugly bodies.

Not surprisingly rabbinic anecdotes overlap very closely with both the Biblical texts and Greco-Roman attitudes exactly on the general suspicion that women are likely to engage in magic. As we will see below, rabbis are also willing to adopt some distinct Greco-Roman attitudes towards women which appear in some ways to contradict their own ideas, but which assume special female powers. In addition, women suffer in rabbinic literature from a double-barreled vulnerability to the charge of witchcraft, since a rabbinic slant is added to Biblical and Greco-Roman prejudices. In order to understand the particular rabbinic slant, we must turn for a moment to rabbinic methods of argumentation and place the witchcraft statements in this context.

The Talmud is dotted with statements about the specific ability needed by someone who wishes to serve on the Sanhedrin, the Highest Court. One of the most famous is "No one is given a seat on the Sanhedrin unless he can make the unclean insect pure from the Torah" (bSanh 17a). At issue in our discussion is not so much the historical Sanhedrin as the question of the qualifications of a potential member.

This Talmudic citation is transparent to us. That is, the rabbis state as clearly as they could that becoming an expert involves learning a mode of argumentation. The student of the system must learn how to join in these arguments just as becoming an expert in our legal system involves learning the rules.[10]

This system contrasts greatly with the Biblical strategies even when it overlaps in content. Scriptural purity laws declare a set of fluids and the people emitting them unclean by their very nature (along with a number of other types of objects animate and inanimate).[11] Women's bodily functions are unclean, and therefore their exclusion vis-à-vis the cult "natural." This system is not directed at women, and menstruating women simply take their place among other impure people and objects.[12] Women are unclean in what seems a highly factual way; it is simply the way the world works. The rules by which the classification is made are not made clear, much to the chagrin of modern scholars who try to understand the basis for classification.[13]

The rabbis (among many) then reinterpret the Biblical purity system in the face of shifting worldviews, historical realities and the destruction of the Temple. It is not so much the details of the rabbinic system that interest us, as the basic contours of their system. It sets up complex methods for arguing about the classification of unclean/clean. Simply put, they conventionalize the impurity system with rulings and rules, which must be mastered. Learning to work with the rules epitomizes mastery. An expert in the system can argue a case either way![14]

In this conventionalizing system women are excluded from learning the rules whereby they might be able to declare themselves clean. Similarly they cannot learn how to construct for their benefit the classification of actions or people as magical, which is also explicitly stated to be a criterion for joining the Sanhedrin.

We have already seen that the rabbinic system of classification of certain acts as magic had tremendous leeway in drawing lines between the permissible and the impermissible.[15] Rabbinic anecdotes about females who engage in witchcraft demonstrate this leeway and the double-disadvantage for women. The daughters of Rabbi Nahman had the unusual skill of being able to stir a pot with their bare arms (bGit 45a). This skill is mentioned with some puzzlement that women should have such a skill, including a citation from Qohelct 7:28 "One man in a thousand have I found, but a woman among all those I have not found." An appended story recounts that these women were carried off into captivity where a fellow Jew overhears them saying that they prefer their new husbands and do not want to be rescued. This individual, when he returns to the Jews, clearly states that their unusual power was based on witchcraft. The women's ability is not classified as witchcraft until it has been thoroughly investigated. Only when the women were found to be wanting as wives were they declared to be witches. Perhaps the point here is that since the women were attached to a rabbinic family the status of their deeds was an open question, until their moral failings settled it.

Attitudes towards menstrual blood embody the over determined attitudes towards women. That is, the rabbis are willing to make use of any and even contradictory negative evaluations of menstrual blood. Thus, while Cohen (1991) argues that the menstruant only begins to be perceived as a real threat to those around her in the sixth or seventh century, all the parts of the puzzle were already in place in the first centuries. The conventionalizing of the purity laws, and the exclusion of women from the process, had been going on for centuries. Menstrual blood, unlike other types of blood such as the blood spilled during circumcision, is unclean (Hoffman 1996: 172). The contagion of impurity was a constant threat for rabbis and the limits of the contagion had to be discussed in detail.

In addition, along with the standard notions of impure menstrual blood the rabbis appear to have borrowed attitudes towards menstrual blood from the general culture. Numerous Greco-Roman writers mention the special powers of menstrual blood. Pliny listed all the powers of this blood as part of his discussion of a variety of female fluids that are thought to have special properties (urine, spit, etc.).

> Contact with it turns new wine sour, crops touched by it become barren, grafts die, seeds in gardens are dried up, the fruit of trees falls off, the bright surface of mirrors in which it is merely reflected is dimmed, the edge of steel and the gleam of ivory are dulled, hives of bees die, even bronze and iron are at once seized with rust.
>
> (*NH* 7.64–5)

The power of menstrual blood can be put to work positively, as well. According to Pliny, menstrual blood can be used to undo other people's spells (*NH* 28.70–1). Tacitus learned from ancient sources that it could be used to get sticky bitumen off the bottom of boats.[16] The usefulness of women's rags in averting hail crops up in Plutarch (*QuesCon* 7.1–2).[17] Josephus tells us that it can be used to uproot a particularly lethal plant used in exorcisms (*BJ* 7.180–5). For Columella its most important task is to help with infested olives. Infested crops can be cured by a menstruating woman who walks three times around, barefoot, after which the vermin will fall to the ground (*RR* 11.3.64). This idea is attributed to Democritus' treatise *On Antipathies*, taking us back to the natural writers discussed above in Chapter 4.

Belief in the power of menstrual blood conveys a special power to women in general. A woman even when she is not menstruating can prevent a storm (*NH* 7.64) and even a female glance, in the right circumstances, can kill (*NH* 2.17).

The rabbis knew of these ideas. Uses of menstrual blood by the general public are hinted at in rabbinic texts that refer to menstrual rags traded for their powers. The fame of Rekem for its menstrual rags is taken for granted in a midrash which compares taking straw to Afarayim with taking bloodstains to Rekem (*Tanhuma Vayera* Buber 12). Most surprisingly is that these ideas appear side by side with purity issues, even though they are at variance with them. A ruling blithely declares that "All stains that come from Rekem are clean" (mNid 7:3).[18] Idol-worshippers are exempt from the rules of purity, thus their stains are not impure. These stains are classified with other types of female blood which are not impure, such as blood spilled in blood-letting, hymenal blood and blood from a genital wound (mNid 1.7,1.9,10.1, bNid 17b). These ideas do not explain the Rekem ruling, since it includes stains of Jewish women, a confusion leading some early commentators to emend the text (bNid 56b). Lieberman therefore argued that the Mishnah was influenced by Greco-Roman ideas about menstrual blood (1965: 102).

It is in this context – Greco-Roman notions of the power of menstrual blood – that we must understand rabbinic claims that seem at variance with their standard notions of impurity, how it is conveyed, and its impact. None of their standard notions can explain the striking claim made in the Talmud that a menstrual woman passing between two men can kill them if it is the onset of her menses or simply cause strife between them if it is the end (bPes 111a). Such a statement makes no sense in terms of rabbinic notions of impurity.

We find other instances when Greco-Roman principles seem to be freely adapted to rabbinic beliefs about women and magic. In two anecdotes a woman is held up by her tresses in order to diminish her power, pointing to some type of belief in the chthonic power of women. In the first one, the story is recounted in such a condensed version that it is impossible to make sense of the story without filling in many gaps. A women is presumed to be hindering a man from having children, and when she is hoisted up by her hair declares that she cannot do anything since something of hers is at the bottom of the ocean. The word for the missing object is itself missing or repressed in the text; translations usually supply a phrase such as "magical material." The rabbi then retrieves the missing item, whatever it is and the man, or presumably his wife, is able to bear children (jSanh 7.13).

This anecdote intersects with a set of anecdotes about Simeon ben Shetah who goes out to a cave to combat the 80 women living there.[19] In some versions of the story the women are simply referred to as women, in some they are specifically called "women who engage in witchcraft." Shetah defeats the women by bringing 80 men for them (this part of the story has clear sexual overtones), each of whom hoists up a woman so that she loses her power. Shetah is thereby able to hang them all in one day. In these two stories women must be connected to the earth in order to have their power.

Women, in fact, have a great deal of power attributed to them in these stories of conflict. They can change shape,[20] mirroring the ability of daimons to take on the shape of animals. Women can cast spells with their eyes, a skill some men also have (*Pesikta* 90b). Rabbis and men in general must be equipped with all sorts of formulas to recite when they encounter unknown women, lest they fall under their power.

These rabbinic stories, dramatic as they are, fail to illuminate any lost or repressed religious and social roles. As mentioned above, what is called "magic" is sometimes the carrying on of older religious rituals in the face of social and theological changes. Some of the Biblical denunciations of witches may hint at actual religious roles women fulfilled as, for example diviners. Jeremiah 7:18, for example, denounced women who continued to worship the Queen of Heaven long after the author thought such practices should have ended. The denunciations help us reconstruct the lost practice.

For this type of evidence, the rabbinic anecdotes are disappointing. Rabbinic anecdotes imply that there were sisterhoods of witches with their own hierarchy, figures such as the head of witches Ameimar encountered (bPes 110a). But these groups seem very ephemeral even in the anecdotes themselves. Most of the "witches" whom rabbis confronted head-to-head are individual women, both Jewish and non-Jewish, who they encountered and opposed in what seem to be impromptu settings. A woman is refused a seat on a boat and therefore curses a rabbi (bShab 81b). A Gentile woman curses Rabbi Judah's ship so that he has to put his clothes in water, thereby partially fulfilling and thus averting the curse (bBabaB 153a).

The only possible social roles disguised in charges of witchcraft are healing and midwifery roles.[21] A condensed story refers to "prying widows" who bring about the destruction of the world (bSota 22a). Among these is Johani daughter of Retibi, though no explanation at all is given as to what she did. Rashi explains that Johani was a witch who could delay the onset of childbirth in women, and then offer prayers which would appear to bring on labor.[22] It is very tempting to see some twisted reference to midwifery in this anecdote.

In a number of anecdotes rabbis turn to female family members for help with illnesses, help which borders so close on what would be called "magic" in other circumstances that the permissive tone of the anecdotes is striking. These remedies might include the foodstuffs found in kitchens, the use of amulets and the recitation of formulas or Biblical verses. In one set of anecdotes Abaye, for example, reveals some of the cures advocated by his stepmother, and even her antidote against witchcraft of seven garlands of garlic (bShab 66b).

These women are permitted to show their knowledge since the women are presented as family members, who operate within the sphere of the family. Their cures can also be permitted under the ruling that anything which helps people is not magic. They are not presented as experts in supernatural knowledge in general but as experts in how to deal with witches since they are of the same gender. Their power is extremely limited. In one revealing anecdote Rabbi Yohanan learns the ingredients for a cure for scurvy from a matron and then, after promising her not to reveal the ingredients, does so anyway. The story, which appears in several versions, has more than one ending.[23] In one she chokes on a bone and dies and in the other she converts to Judaism. The woman's identity varies from version to version – in one she refuses to heal on the Sabbath – but the one constant is the theft of the cure by the rabbi.

While any woman who had a major religious role would likely be denounced as a witch by the rabbis, the reverse is not true, that every woman denounced as a witch was fulfilling some recognized religious role. Evidence for long-lost religious roles of women is not found in the rabbinic stories.[24]

We do in fact find a few cases of Greco-Roman women who were experts in esoteric traditions and present the flip-side of charges of being a witch, though they take us past our central period of interest. First to come to mind is Hypatia, the Greco-Roman mathematician and philosopher stoned by a Christian crowd as a witch. The case of another female philosopher Sosipatra, with a happier ending, is recounted by Eunapius in his *Lives of the Philosophers* 466–471 (mid-fourth century). Her dramatic story begins when two men visit her family, and impressed by the daughter, tell the parents that they are "initiates into Chaldean wisdom" and that their daughter is "equal to divinity." They are revealed to be daimons and she is apprenticed to them for a period during which they are her teachers. When they subsequently disappear as mysteriously as they came, they leave her gifts including garments, books, and mysterious items. She goes on to live the life of a great philosopher (greater than her husband) surrounded by a small group of disciples. She could predict the future, bi-locate and "it was said that concerning the gods, nothing happened without her being there to see" (470).

Maria the Jewess is the closest Jewish figure we have found to compare to Hypatia and Sosipatra. She, too, may have had a small circle of disciples who turned to her based on her reputation for secret knowledge. Maria, in addition to being earlier than either of these women, also worked with pans, fires and complex mixtures of metals. Perhaps the few exceptional women who were engaged in primarily theoretical investigation only prove the point that women are usually relegated to practical questions.[25]

The crowd's fatal imaginings about Hypatia were far from the perceptions such women had about themselves. Maria the Jewess and her complex distillation devices were so far from the worldview of the rabbis that they do not even bother to denounce her. If a decent woman is full of witchcraft, it is hard to imagine a suitable term in their eyes for a woman who thought she could lay bare the secret processes of the world and speed them on their way by heating metals over a stove. Instead in rabbinic literature we remain imprisoned in the fertile imaginations of the rabbis, where it is equally dangerous to walk between two women, palm trees, dogs, or, some say, pigs (bPes 111a). Pairs were generally thought to be unlucky in the Greco-Roman world, and palm trees were thought to be home to daimons. Women find them classified with animals such as pigs and dogs, placing them by nature and by convention at a tremendous disadvantage. Biblical prejudices merge with Greco-Roman ones, filter through rabbinic anxieties about women's unclean bodies and it is possible to see every woman as a potential witch. These imaginings were not always acted upon, but they are part of the artifice of magic bequeathed to later generations.

CONCLUDING NOTE

The legacy of the first centuries

The point of this study is not that magic is simply another term for religion. It is true that ancient practitioners considered much of what modern scholars label magic to simply be their religion. But this observation hardly begins to articulate the rich imaginings about magic in the first three centuries CE, which deserve to be examined in their own right.

Notions of magic were developed at length by numerous writers, given detailed nuances and debated. From the minor theme of fraud to the more threatening themes of cannibalism and murder, the activities of magicians were understood to threaten society in general. Witches might prey upon total strangers and innocent children, or more close to home, unsuspecting family members.

Everyday life presented endless chances for getting caught up in the magical powers of one's opponents. In a rabbinic anecdote, a woman complains that she has no power over certain rabbis since they did not wipe themselves with a shard, kill lice on vessels or untie and eat vegetables from a bunch (bShab 81b–82a). All of these seemingly innocent actions might have made them vulnerable to her powers.

With Pliny, we saw the tremendous plasticity of the term "magic" as a space-holder for practices far from those originally associated with the Persian priests. In a world in which the criteria for establishing the validity of a cure were thin, Pliny tried to differentiate his material from a vast array of (in his eyes) fraudulent offerings. Pliny reinforced the validity of his writings by denouncing both doctors, who used their social status to gain wealth, and the "fraudulent vanities" of the magi who mixed astronomy in their cures.

After "magic" was written into the Roman law codes, it would have required an antiquarian bent to use the term with its more ancient connotations. In most cases, as we saw above, it had acquired too many negative associations in Greek and later Latin literature for the positive connotations associated with the ancient Persian magi to survive.

The rituals we studied (exorcism, love rites, alchemy, and deification) all point to the importance of the first three centuries. Ideas which appeared only in embryonic form before the turn of the millennium undergo tremendous development by the beginning of the fourth century. Many of these rites echo much older ideas, such as ancient notions of possession. They all, however, have distinct connections with the particular setting of the first centuries. They all had an implicit gounding in the notions that on the one hand life on earth is a series of intimate battles between good and evil forces and on the other that it was possible for humans to achieve a divine status, sometimes even while alive. Possession permitted the daimonic forces to be bodily manifest on earth and then subjected to personal defeat. Love rites in turn made use of ancient ideas about sacrifice, now directed to the angelic and daimonic helpers whose task it was to assist humans in their struggles. These rites could draw upon a plethora of ideas about effective words and objects to help ensure success. Alchemical rites turned nostalgically to the natural world, yet also aimed at divine transformations. Deification rites drew new boundaries for human identity, enabling human hands to "make power."

After reviewing the evidence for Jewish witches in the Greco-Roman period Tal Ilan concludes, "Actual witches we do not meet at all in this period" (1996: 225). "Witch" was not a term of self-identification in the first three centuries CE, and given the gruesome literary portraits of witches it is not hard to see why. It was a term of fantasy, used in imaginative and usually hostile depictions of women. The rabbinic system of conventionalization made it all the more over-determined that women would be witches. Women could theoretically have declared that they did magic only for the purpose of study, but the paths to this kind of power were not open to them.

Overall the criteria used in classifying actions and beliefs as "magic" were not tradition-specific; people from a wide variety of religious traditions shared them. So too in each chapter we saw that similar rituals were found in different traditions, with both similar goals and means. Maria and Zosimos had more in common with each other than with other practitioners within their own traditions.

Past scholars have diminished the importance of these parallels by stressing that people were only borrowing magic, which was understood to be degraded religion. These borrowings no longer look so degraded, and thus force us to rethink our notions of religious boundaries. Nor was this an issue only in the general populace where amulets reflected the international language of power in the first centuries. Elites from various settings put great effort into keeping esoteric traditions away from both their particular *hoi polloi* and from competing elites. Numerous anecdotes present various rabbinic figures as prodigious supernatural powers in their own right, as was noted already decades ago by Jacob Neusner (1969). As such, rabbis were in conflict with other figures who, like themselves, wielded special power. Rabbis compete with necromancers (bBer 59a), dream interpreters, the mysterious but powerful "men of deed," and, last but not least, women.

If we can no longer equate a certain set of rituals with magic, it simultaneously becomes harder to separate out the normative from the heretical. Normative religion needs to be broadly enough defined to include the early alchemical traditions as well as divinization rites, and then also rites for success in love. Even those who rejected the more dramatic rhetoric of divinization had as their ultimate goal to become part of the heavenly, immortal world and not the earthly mortal one; this is an inherent redrawing of the more ancient human/divine boundary.

As to the practitioners, even though the texts are not clearly labeled as the property of Rabbi X or Bishop Y, there is no doubt that all sorts of religious authorities, some known to us and many lost, made use of the various rituals described throughout this study. These would not be instances of magic, since, as we learned, authorities cannot – by definition – engage in magic. They can, however, bless, curse, heal, exorcise, predict the future, and put angels to work.

In 1999 the last remaining Jew in Kabul, Afghanistan was charged with being a magician, playing out a stereotype set in the first centuries.[1] Jews have been vulnerable to all that comes with being thought to have special, secret knowledge, and charges of engaging in "magic" haunted Jews for centuries. The charges did not continue to haunt pagans since their modes of religious practices died out or were taken over by Christians. Pagan practices adopted by Christians are still often mis-characterized as the "magical" component of Christianity (Flint 1991). This too is ironic, since the negative valuation of "magic" was originally a product of Greek writers. They would be shocked and dismayed to find that Greco-Roman priests and philosophers came to be called magicians by Christians.

Ancient polemical stance continues in many guises, such as comments that monotheism is by nature less hospitable to "magic" than polytheism. Egypt continues to loom large in the modern imagination of magic; just about any material object used in Egyptian religious rituals is likely to be labeled "magical object" in museums today.

The more we understand those imaginings, the better we are able to trace their lingering impacts today and decide if these are imaginings we wish to embrace.

NOTES

Introduction

1 For accusations connecting ritual murder and magic see also Cicero, *inVat* 6.14 and Pliny, *NH* 30.3. For charges of necromancy and the gathering of body parts from corpses, see Horace, *Sat* 1.8, and Lucan, *BelCiv* 6.499ff. Depictions of witches are also discussed in Chapter 6.
2 See most recently Burrus 1995.
3 See Tamsyn Barton's comments about the distinct social roles of astrology in the ancient and modern worlds (1994).
4 A few exceptions are discussed in Chapter 1.
5 Points of entry into the extensive anthropological discussions of this term range from Hammond 1970 to Tambiah 1990. For the implications for the study of religion, see J. Z. Smith 1978b: 190–207; 1995: 17–18 and Neusner *et al.* 1989.
6 These laws are presented most succinctly in the introductory chapter of *The Golden Bough*.
7 See Tambiah 1990 for a lucid critique of Edmund Tylor and James Frazer.
8 mTa'anit 3:8, bTa'anit 23a, bBer 34b and parallels, as well as Josephus, *Ant* 14.22. See Bokser 1985.
9 For an analysis of how Honi's power is "rabbinized," see William Scott Green 1975.
10 See Hildred Geertz' illuminating critique of Keith Thomas' attempt to salvage the term "magic" (1975).
11 See the collection of essays and extensive bibliography in Krausz 1989.
12 See the recent book by Vyse 1997.

Greco-Roman, Christian and Jewish concepts of "magic"

1 See de Jong 1997: 387–413 for an extensive discussion of the term.
2 Kingsley 1995.

3 Nock 1972: 308–33; Graf 1997:20–60.
4 The first term comes from *Vodu,* the word for spirit or deity in the language of the Fon people who live in Dahomey; the second term refers to a Hindi or Muslim holy man.
5 Heraclitus classified them with wanderers of the night (Clement of Alexandria, *Protrep* 22). Cf. Graf 1997: 21–4.
6 See Burkert 1962. Centuries later Augustine still commented on the "more detestable name" of *goetia* (*CivDe* 10.9).
7 For other positive uses of the term "magi", see Nock 1972: 17 n. 20.
8 Cf. *De spec Leg* 3.100.
9 Compare this with Clement's positive comment that the magi were able to foretell the savior's birth (*Strom* 1.15).
10 Pharr 1932 and Kippenberg 1995.
11 For discussions of this code, see Kippenberg 1995: 149–50 and Honoré 1996.
12 See Iulius Paulus, *Sententiae* V.23.14–18.
13 Kippenberg 1995: 149.
14 Kippenberg 1995: 140 mentions an increase in charges during the first century under Tiberius and during the second half of the fourth century under Constantius II, Valentinian I and Valens. This increase in charges does not mean that there was more "magic." The particular contours of social conflict were distinct in the two periods, as Kippenberg himself intimates.
15 *CodTheo* 9.16.1–2. Cf. Pharr 1932: 281–6.
16 Pharr 1932: 277ff. and Graf 1997: 41–2.
17 Kippenberg 1995: 144–7.
18 Pharr 1932: 277.
19 Pharr 1932: 279.
20 See also Theocritus 2.15; Cicero, *ProCluentio* 148; Virgil, *Ecl* 8.95; Pliny, *NH* 25.26; Lucan, *BelCiv* 6.681–4.
21 Pharr 1932: 272–5.
22 The specific charges appear to have been *magica maleficia* (*Apol* 1.15) and *crimen magiae* (*Apol* 25.14). See Kippenberg 1995: 141–7.
23 This topic is discussed below.
24 On Thrace see Pliny, *NH* 30.7. On Thessaly, see Horace, *Ode* 1.27, 21–2; *Epistle* 2.2.208–9; Tibullus 2.4.55–60; Ovid, *Amores* 1.14.39–40 and 3.7.27–30; *ArsAmat* 2.99–104; *RemAm* 249–52; Seneca, *Phaedra* 420–23 and 790–2; *Medea* 787–811; *HerOet* 465–72 and 523–7; Valerius Flavius 1.735–38, 6.445–8, 7.198–99 and 7.325–30; Pliny *NH* 30.6–7; Statius, *Theb* 3.557–9; and Apuleius, *Meta* 2.1. See in addition specific references to the witches of Thessaly in Chapter 6.
25 See for example the treatise on sympathy written by Proclus and translated into English in Copenhaver 1988.
26 Copenhaver 1988.
27 Whether or not these writings constitute the origins of modern medicine is a question beyond this study. For a lucid statement of the

problems with simpler cultural genealogies from the ancient to modern world, see Tamsyn Barton 1994.

28 Cf. pages 25–6 below and Simon 1986: 361–2.
29 See John Chysotom *inPs.* 8:3 (*PG* 55:110), the uncensored version of bSanh 43a, tHullin 2:20 and parallels as well as the discussion by M. Smith 1978: 46–50.
30 For the standard equation of paganism and magic found in the writings of the Christian apologists, see Thee 1984: 328. Cf. Ps.-Clementine, *Hom* 5.4–7; Clement, *Protrep* 1 and *Paed* 3.4.
31 For Christian rituals that looked magical to pagans, see for example Suetonius *Nero* 16.2 and the comments of Celsus preserved by Origen in *Contra Celsum*.
32 This common claim is also discussed in Chapter 2.
33 The treatise was written in the 240s, probably in 248. Translations from *Contra Celsum* are taken from Chadwick's edition.
34 See Chapter 2 for a more detailed discussion of the various supernatural figures.
35 For a modern repetition of this claim, see Thee who states that there is "no real boundary between magic and pagan worship." He accepts the Christian polemics that they do not engage in magic, stating "In essence, magic did not 'fit' in the Christian world-view while it was a natural counterpart of the pagan religion" (1984: 345).
36 Traditions about healing songs are found in Homer, the Derveni papyrus' reference to the songs of the magi, the scrolls found at Qumran (*Apocryphl Psalms* (*11QPsa*) 27:9) and the rabbinic stories about "Songs of the Stricken" (bSheb 15b; jErub 10.11 and jShab 6.2).
37 Here again Origen follows other early Christian writers such as Irenaeus.
38 For recent theoretical discussions of rabbis and magic which struggle with the dilemma, see Alexander 1986; Schäfer 1990; Swartz 1990; 1996; and Kern-Ulmer 1996.
39 The recent article by Kuemmerlin-McLean 1992 is more nuanced than most. See also Baruch Levine's comment about the nature of Biblical injunctions against magic (1974: 89).
40 For Biblical citations see Deut 18:10–11; Lev 19:26, 31; 20:1–6; 27; Exod 22:18; Isa 47:9–15; 2 Kings 21:6, 9:22; 2 Chron 33:6; Mic 5:11; Jer 29:9; Mal 5:3; Nah 3:4; Ezek 13:17–23; Jer 8:17; Ps 58:6; Qoh 10:11. For "bad" kings who practiced magic see 2 Kings 21:6.
41 Translations from Schmidt 1994:179.
42 Similarly self-mutilation was permitted until the sixth century BCE (Schmidt 1994: 287).
43 Jer 27:9–10, 29:8–9; Zech 10:2; and Ezek 12:24.
44 Compare raising the dead with a skull discussed in the text and raising the dead without a skull discussed in bBabaK 117a. See also jSan 7.10.
45 For capital punishment for female witches compare Ex 22:17 and rabbinic texts discussed in Chapter 6.
46 It is impossible to give a simple date for this discussion. We can,

however, point out that many of the same themes are found in parallel Christian and Greco-Roman texts which are datable to the first three centuries, as noted throughout this discussion.

47 Contrast Urbach's reading of the ruling as a comment that only magicians who take their work seriously are liable (1975: 100) with Levinas' recent interpretation that magic is important only when it has economic consequences (1994: 142).

48 The role of intention is central in many other rabbinic discussions.

49 See Pharr's comment that ancient authorities claimed that only the practice not the knowledge was prohibited (1932: 293).

50 For a discussion of these laws, see Barb 1963: 106, Kippenberg 1995: 149–50.

51 Healings are attributed both to rabbis and to women associated with rabbinical families. See Chapter 6.

52 Attributed to Rabbi Johanan.

53 For further discussion of this topic, see Chapter 6.

54 See the contest between Jannai and a woman in bSanh 67b.

55 bShab 67a, tShab 6–7 in the name of Abbaye and Rava. Lieberman 1936: I.126–7; 1955: 74ff.

56 Goldin 1963: 118 and Lieberman 1955: 83.

57 Goldin 1963: 118 and Lieberman 1955: 88.

58 Goldin 1963: 118 and Lieberman 1955: 82.

59 bShab 67a. Cf. bNid 66a.

60 See the discussion by Lieberman 1965: 103.

61 Zosimos, the compiler of late antique alchemical texts discussed below in Chapter 4, had an especially high opinion of Jewish alchemical writings and preserved anything he found attributed to Jews.

62 These ancient equations led a generous number of scholars (such as Simon 1986) to argue that late antique magic was in fact a product of Judaism.

63 See also Juvenal 6.542–7.

64 Rawson notes, for example, that there is no evidence that during the Republic people turned to Jews for magical aid (1985: 309).

Daimons and angels and the world of exorcism

1 bKid 29b. In this story a seven-headed daimon appeared to the overnight guest.

2 bHul 105b. Cf. bShab 81b–82a.

3 bHul 105b.

4 For introductory discussions of angels and daimons see Kohler 1901; Cumont 1907; Michl 1962; Colpe 1978; Newson 1992; and Riley 1992.

5 See, for example, the extended presentation of fallen angels in 1 Enoch 6–8 and also *Pirqe R. El* 22.

6 See *GenRab* 24; *LevRab* 28.3, 5.

7 bBer 3a, bHul 105b; and *Tanhuma Mishpatim* 19.

8 According to Celsus the Jews worship the heavens and angels (*CC* 5.6).
9 Gen 32:1; Job 25:3; Josh 5:13–15; 1 Kings 22:19.
10 Gen 3:24; 1 Sam 4:4; Ps 80:2; 98(99):1.
11 Gen 16:11; 21:17; 31:11–13; Ex 3:2–6; Num 22:22, 31 and Jud 2:1.
12 See M. Barker's discussion, though her differentiation between Elohim and Yahweh remains controversial (1992).
13 Gen 18:2, 19:5; Jud 6:17, 13:6. Some creatures were hybrid human and animal forms, such as the Seraphim, Cherubim and Se'irim.
14 Texts which describe the multi-layered heavens range from the Enoch texts, which pre-date our period of interest, to the much later esoteric rabbinic discussion found in tractate Hagigah.
15 Bickerman and Smith 1976: 14.
16 Cumont 1907: 166 and Nilsson 1946.
17 Cf. Oenomaus in Eusebius, *PE* 5:21 (213B).
18 1 Enoch 19:1 and Philo, *de Decal* 74.
19 Peter Brown 1978: 151.
20 See also Euripides' comment that good mortals became daimons (*Alc* 1003).
21 LXX Ps 96 95:4ff. and LXX Deut 32:17.
22 See especially *deIsis* 25–6 and *deDefectu* 10–21.
23 Noted by J. Z. Smith 1978a. For a modern re-use of the Persian theory see Kohut 1866.
24 *Il* 3.420 for Aphrodite, a usage that is still found in Acts 17:18.
25 Among the most important texts is *Symposium* 202d–203a.
26 *Epinomis* 984ef on the hierarchy of beings.
27 For additional discussions of the daimons, see Maximus of Tyre 8–9 (86–110); Porphyry, *deAbstin* 27–42; Ps-Clementine, *Homilies* 8–9; *Recognitions* 4 and Apuleius, *deDogmaPlat* 1.12.
28 See Apuleius' extensive discussion in *deDeoSoc* 6–9.
29 For important points about daimons see *InPlatRemp* II, p. 271, 21 Kroll; *InCratyl* 128, p. 75, 9ff. Pasquali; *InPlatRemp* II, p. 345, 1 Kroll; *InTim* III p. 140, 26ff. Diehl; and *InPlatRemp* II p. 255, 23ff. Kroll.
30 *InCratyl* 74, p. 98, 21, Pasquali.
31 This text is discussed at greater length in Chapter 3.
32 See, for example, bGitten 68b where a daimon inhabits a male body in order to have intercourse with women. For men, intercourse with female daimons, see *Tanhuma* Buber Appendix p. 6.
33 Kapferer 1979: 156. See also Corin 1998.
34 Comparisons will only be improved when, as Ruth Padel argues, we are not comparing isolated metaphors but more developed models (1983).
35 Brown 1978: 25.
36 Brown 1998: 30–1.
37 Vermes 1995: 69–89 has a complete translation of the text which is thought to be among the earliest documents in the library, dating perhaps to 100 BCE. We do not know if anyone ever attempted to live by these rules when the texts were composed. We do have rich evi-

dence of later church orders which reflect similar themes and were used in monastic communities.

38 The date of the Book of Acts is disputed and thus the dating for this use of the term. For discussion, see Munck 1967.

39 These formulas are discussed at greater length in Chapter 3.

40 Mark 3:11, 5:7–8; Luke 4:34, 8:28.

41 The exorcism discussed below also includes blowing air on the possessed person from his foot to his head.

42 See Bonner 1927; Knox 1930; and Thraede 1969.

43 See the now-classic work by Austin 1962 which has influenced many studies, among which is Tambiah 1968.

44 For a more detailed discussion, see Janowitz 2001 and the bibliography cited there.

45 See bSuc 28a and Clement, *Strom.* 1.21.

46 See Pliny, *NH* 28.6; Clement, *Strom* 1.15 and 5.8; and *PGM* 7.532. For additional citations and discussion, see McCown 1923 and Bonner 1946: 29–30.

47 Compare bKid 81b and bMeil 17b.

48 For the use of Jesus' name in exorcisms, see Mark 9:38, Luke 9:49, Origen, *CC* 1.6, 1.25, 6.40; Irenaeus, *AdHaer* 2.5; and in rabbinic literature tHullin 2:22–23; jShab 14.4; jAZ 2.2, bAZ 27b; and *LamRab* Buber 5:16. See Geller 1977: 146ff.

49 Compare Luke 4:34–6 where Jesus rebuked him "Be silent and come out of him." In Jude 9 Michael promises the devil that the "Lord will rebuke you."

50 The Greek texts were edited by Preisendanz in 1931 and a second edition prepared by Henrichs 1973. English translation is found in Betz 1986: 44–6.

51 Knox 1930 divides the exorcism into two sections, the first 3033–45 where the goal is for the daimon to speak, and the second 3045–78 where the daimon does not speak, with a concluding section 3078–end.

52 See below, pages 56–7.

53 For similar summaries, see Jud 5:5–19; Philo, *VitCon* 11; Josephus, *Ant* 2.12–16 and 3.17. For a discussion of this type of historical summary, see Frankfurter 1995.

54 For discussion, see Duling 1985.

55 Among them the Galilean amulet from the third century CE mentioned by Duling 1975: 244 n. 39.

56 See Perdrizet 1903 and Goodenough 1963: 1.68, 2.226–38, 7.198–200 and 9.1044–67.

57 Duling 1975: 245ff.

58 See McCown 1922: 5.

59 Additional stories about Asmodeus appear in *TestSolo* 5:1–13; bGit 78a; bPes 110a; and in bBer 6a where he rules in place of King Solomon for a while.

60 bGit 68a. Cf. *PesRab* 15.

61 Another pilgrim, also from the fourth century, saw the cave where Solomon tortured the daimons (McCown 1922: 23).
62 See Knox 1930: 202–3.
63 For dating and bibliography see Carey Moore 1996. As described here the text seems most likely to pre-date the first century CE.
64 Modified sacrifices are discussed below in Chapter 3, page 53.
65 Tertullian, *AdScap* 4; Hippolytus, *AposCon* 20ff.
66 This point is discussed by J. Z. Smith 1978a.
67 For exceptions, see Marcus Aurelius, *Med* 1.6; and Plotinus, *Enn* 2.9.14, as well as Lucan.

Ancient rites for gaining lovers

1 Cited according to firmament and line number following Morgan 1983. Hence this rite appears in line 31 of the Second Firmament.
2 Scholars who label the text "magic" include Margalioth 1966; Dan 1967: 208–114; Maier 1968; Niggemeyer 1975; Gruenwald 1980: 225–34; Schäfer 1990; Morgan 1983; and Swartz 1990.
3 See Introduction note 8 and mSotah 9:5, Avot 5.6, *GenRab* 5.5; and Bokser 1985: 42.
4 In a variant reading the text is given to Adam.
5 See, for example, the reference to a Noahic book of healing in Jubilees 10:13.
6 Rituals which confirm an elevated status for the practitioner are discussed in Chapter 5.
7 In *The Book of Secrets* healing rituals are found at 1.29, 2.95 and 2.182. Both 1.94 and 5.15 are directed at learning about the future.
8 Alexander supplements Margalioth's discussion, adding that the indiction method of counting years began in 312, with a five year indiction in Egypt perhaps as early as 287; the use of this method in "non-fiscal contexts" did not begin until the second half of the fourth century (1986: 348 n.15). The text lacks the paleographical evidence crucial in dating Greek papyri (Morgan 1983: 8).
9 This is the same formula as found in the exorcism discussed in Chapter 2.
10 *ShirRab* 7.8. Cf. Lieberman 1965: 107–8.
11 See, for example, *PGM* 2.110.
12 See Lieberman 1955 3: 103–4; 1965: 97, 100–14.
13 No clay bowls dating to the first three centuries have been found; most are from the fifth to the seventh centuries.
14 In some versions it is R. Johanan. Cf. Lieberman 1974: 24.
15 See Chapter 2, page 31.
16 Cf. *ExMar* 45. The specific reference to offerings here is from Homer, *Il* iv. 49; ix. 50; xxiv. 70.
17 See also 1 Enoch 19.
18 Lauterbach is probably correct that this practice was the basis for the

popular Tashlich service where individuals cast bread into a body of water for forgiveness of sins (1936). See for example the reference to worshipping the Ruler of the Sea in bHullin 41b and to the Ruler of the Sea following Rabbi Joshua's orders in jSanh7.13. The practice of throwing something into a lake is also denounced as a Way of the Amorites (tShab 6.1).

19 The statue of a lion is used in 2.18.

20 The injunction against images Exod 20:4-5a is supplemented by Ex 20:23, 34:17; Lev 19:4, 26:1; Deut 4:15–19, 25:5–8. For Christian adoption of this language, see Acts 17:16 and 19:24–41.

21 For the use of images in Israelite religion, see Ex 32–34; Jud 8:26–27, 17–18; 1 Kings 12:28–33; 2 Kings 18:4; 21:1–7; Hos 3:4; and I Sam 19:13. The iconography of the deity's consort, the Asherah, is so repressed that it is remembered only as a wooden pole.

22 See Herodotus, *Hist* 4.62, Ammianus Marcellinus 31.2.23 and Xenophanes cited above.

23 See Majercik 1989: 26–7; Lewy 1978: 230–8; Dodds 1947: 63.

24 The evidence is gathered in numerous places including Goodenough 1963 and Hachlili 1988.

25 See Lieberman 1962: 121 n. 33.

26 See Xenophanes, *DK* 21B 15016, Heredotus, *Hist* 4.62 and Ammianus Marcellinus 31.2.23.

27 In this vein a recent article on idolatry characterizes the numerous small statues located in what appears to be the context of worship of Yahweh as popular practice or superstition and not formal religion (Curtis 1992).

28 For a more technical discussion of Peircean semiotics, see Janowitz 2001.

29 See Bonner 1950.

30 The modern practice is one box on the left hand and one on the head.

31 Probably composed in the first and second century BCE in Alexandria.

32 Josephus comments on the practice (*Ant* 4.213).

33 See the discussion of the secrecy which surrounds Greek binding spells by Faraone 1991, especially p. 11.

34 Even a scholar as subtle as Alan Segal comments about the use of curses tablets that "No one would have practiced it with the impression he was practicing a legal and wholesome religious rite, however, richly deserved was the damage to the intended victim" (1980: 88–97).

35 For a combination of blessings and curses, see Deut 27–8. On the automatic nature of both blessings and curse, see Gen 27 and Num 22.

Using natural forces for divine goals: Maria the Jewess and early alchemy

1 Forbes 1964: 138 and Lindsay 1970: chaps 5–6 tentatively date him to 200 BCE. See also M. Wellman 1928, Festugière 1950: 197 and

Waszink 1954. He is sometimes conflated with Democritus, under whose name he may have written (Columella, *RR* 7.5.17).

2 A statement of his about menstrual blood is discussed in Chapter 6 page 93.

3 Pliny, *NH* 32.52. Wellman 1928 remains the most important discussion.

4 See Suda, DL 1.10; Eusebius, *PrEv* 3.2; and *Geoponica* 20.6.3.

5 Rawson 1985.

6 Slightly later writers include Pamphilos of Alexandria (first century CE) who wrote a treatise called "Natural Forces" (*Geoponica* 15.1.6; Wellman 1928; Festugière 1950: 197), Xenocrates of Aphrodisia (Wellman 1928; Festugière 1950: 197), a physician in Nero's time, who wrote about natural treatments and Aelius Promotus (second century CE) who also wrote "On Natural Forces" (Wellman 1893).

7 The confusion between Democritus and Bolos means that Bolos is in turn implicated in early alchemy (Taylor 1930: 114–15).

8 For discussion of the term "alchemy," see Forbes 1964: 126 and for numerous possible derivations, many of them fanciful, see Lindsay 1970: 68–89.

9 For introductions to alchemy, see Berthelot 1885; Riess 1893; Festugière 1939, 1950; Taylor 1949; and Forbes 1964.

10 Zosimos wrote before the Serapeum was destroyed in the 390s but cited Africanus who died in 232. On his dates see among others Berthelot 1885: 201 and Festugière 1950: 239. For a concise introduction see Jackson 1978: 7. See Taylor 1937: 88 on his general importance. In general on Zosimos, see Plessner 1976, Riess 1893: 1348; and Hopkins 1934: 69–77. Patai 1994: 51ff. and Lindsay 1970: 323ff. must be used with care. Zosimos' writings are cited by the name of the treatise and numbering in Berthelot's corpus, which is the same for the Greek and the French translation. We cite this edition as Ber. This is a different system of citation than that followed by Patai, who cites the pagination from the French translation, easily confused with the pagination of the Greek original, which he also occasionally cites in error. Later writers cite Maria as well, but these citations raise additional problems about authenticity and thus will not be included.

11 For a brief discussion of the unusual presence of women in early alchemical traditions, see Chapter 6.

12 Lefkowitz and Fant (1992: 299–300) are skeptical that Maria ever existed because the name is common and could be pseudepigraphic. Issues of gender are discussed in Chapter 6.

13 We will return to this point in Chapter 6.

14 See the discussion in Jackson 1978: 3.

15 "On the Letter Omega" is available in English translation in Jackson 1978.

16 Cited by Lippmann 1919: 1.46.

17 On Maria, see Patai 1994:60–91 who cites most of the earlier material.

18 Patai 1994: 60 notes that Zosimos considers "ancient" a treatise on

furnaces, which appears to have been written by Maria. On Maria as Moses' sister, see Patai 1994: 74, which notes that Lippmann offers no support for his claims that this equation was already made by Zosimos.

19 Taylor would date the text to 100 CE (1930: 115; 1937: 32). A "Democritus" is mentioned in the Leiden papyrus, dated approximately 250 CE, making this a possible *terminus ad quem* for the text. Cf. Halleux 1981: 73.

20 See Berthelot 1885: 170–4 and Patai 1994 chapter 4.

21 "On the Letter Omega" 9, Jackson 1978: 29. The same treatise explains that this interpretation was deposited in the Sarapion by Asenas, the high priest of Jerusalem, who sent Hermes to translate the Hebrew Scriptures into Greek and Egyptian. "On the Letter Omega" 8, Jackson 1978: 27.

22 "The First Book of the Final Reckoning," Ber 3.51.3.

23 Similar stories are found in numerous texts. The angels taught women charms, enchantments, the cutting of roots, and taught them about plants (1 Enoch 7) and the fallen angels taught "people making swords, knives, shields, breastplates, and to their chosen ones, bracelets, decorations (eye-shadow) with antimony, ornamentation, beautifying of eyelids, all kinds of precious stones, all coloring tinctures and the 'transmutation of the world' (1 Enoch 8). A recent translation uses the term "alchemy" here, but this is probably an anachronism or a later addition since the term was not in use during the period when most scholars think Enoch was composed. Jubilees discussed the fallen angels but not their specific teachings. See Tertullian, *CultFem* I.2 and II.10 which follows Enoch in much more detail than, for example, Clement, *Strom* 5.1 and Justin *2Apol* 5.

24 Learning the Jewish secrets about metals is hard, according to Zosimos, since they are closely guarded and "nobody either among the Jews or among the Greeks has ever revealed them . . . They are very jealous of divulging the art itself; and they did not let a manipulator remain without punishment." "The First Book of the Final Reckoning," Ber 3.51.3.

25 "Round Alum Must Be Employed," Ber 3.20.6.

26 Olympiodorus "On the Sacred Arts," Ber 2.4.54.

27 The alloy might be silver on the inside too, since it is an alloy of copper, and thus look superior to regular silver (Hopkins 1934: 96).

28 The Greek term can be translated either way.

29 Ps-Democritus "Synesius the Philosopher to Dioscorus," Ber 2.3.6.

30 See Hopkins 1934: 97–8. Taylor 1949: 49–50 believes that this stage could be either further tinting or simply cleaning of the metal or taking away the rust (*ios*).

31 Patai states that Maria said the Great Work could only be done in the Egyptian month of Pharmuti (March–April), that it should be wrapped in linen and boiled in Pontus Water (1994: 64). Here Patai is following Lippmann (1919: 48), who in turn is drawing on Olympiodorus in

Ber. It is not clear from Olympiodorus that these ideas all belong to Maria. I have therefore left them out of consideration here.

32 Cf. Hopkins 1934: 94–95.

33 Forbes mentions descriptions of such devices in Pliny and Dioscorides (1948: 24). It is also referred to by Theophrastus (*De Odor* 22). See Keyser 1990: 362.

34 Forbes adds that there is no evidence of any such apparatus in the Leiden or Stockholm papyri (1948: 21). Nor is it found in Ps-Democritus.

35 Forbes considers and dismisses the possibility that the term refers to the separation of types of distillate into multiple fractions (1948: 23).

36 Taylor (1949: 46–9) states that the closest modern analogy is a reflux extractor.

37 Cf. Taylor 1949: 46–9.

38 Similarly, elsewhere Zosimos writes, "Maria said first, 'The copper cooked with the sulphur, treated by nitre-oil and shaken off frequently undergoing the same treatment, results in a good gold without a shadow'" (Zosimos, "On the Measurement of Yellowing," Ber 3.24.3).

39 "On the Body of Magnesium", Ber 3.28.8.

40 One result of this is that Ruelle substitutes his notion of the "real" name of the substance in the French translation for the name in the Greek, such as "sulphur" for "lead."

41 Zosimos "About the Philosopher's Stone," Ber 3.29.1.

42 Berthelot and Ruelle 1963: 2.1. This treatise is mentioned briefly in Chapter 3.

43 These are all themes familiar from the new cosmology discussed in Chapter 1.

44 Keyser 1990: 360. See also Wellman's claim that magic began with Bolos of Mendes (1928), repeated with some skepticism in Gordon 1987.

45 Hippolytus in his attack on Christian opponents gives away the secret of "*aqua ardens*" in the hope that this will discredit "magicians" and hence his rivals (*Ref* 4.31). This recipe is traced by modern scholars to Anaxilaus and then presented as both proof that magic was in fact thriving in Egypt and that the process of distillation had been invented by those same circles. See Diels 1969: 427–41 following Wellman 1928: 56–62.

46 See also Keyser 1990: 367, 369.

47 Note also the statement that the death of Jesus reduced the daimons to impotence (*CC* 7:17, 8:43; *ComJn* 1.37; cf. *ComJn* 6.36–7).

48 Origen talks about the "natural attraction" of faith and divine power (*ComMatt* 10.19; *PG* 13.884).

49 Tertullian appears to use natural processes to explain how the holy spirit becomes infused in the holy water (*DeBapt* 4).

50 Nock connects the term with the Latin word "*drastike*" often translated as "efficacious" (Nock and Festugière 1950: 232).

51 Betz 1986: 176 n. 39.

Divine power, human hands: becoming gods in the first centuries

1 See the classic discussions by Rohde 1901 II:281 and Wilamowitz-Moellendorff 1959 I.371f.

2 Discussed briefly in Winston 1979: 128. Cf. 4 Ezra 7:97; 2 Baruch 51:10; 4 Macc 17:5; 2 Enoch 66:7; Matt 13:43; *Sifra Deut* 10; and *CII* I, p. 241, no.306.

3 All of these are discussed in detail below except for the role of vegetarianism (Porphyry, *DeAbst* 1.54) and the taurobolium (Prudentius Peristeph, 10/1078).

4 The shift from earthly to heavenly cult is discussed briefly in Chapter 2, page 31.

5 See *Hodayot Hymns* (*1QH*) 6:13, 11:10ff. and *Community Rule* (*1QS*) 11.5–10.

6 See especially the second Song in *4Q ShhirSabb*.

7 See, for example, the fragmentary hymn from 4QH[a] fr.7, sometimes referred to as the "Self-glorification Hymn" which appears to describe explicitly the transformation of a human into a divine being. No doubt as the Qumran texts are scrutinized more closely other examples of merging with angels and transforming of humans will be found.

8 The superiority of some humans over the angels is depicted in rabbinic literature in numerous ways. Angels are described as ranking below humans (bHag 12b, bSanh 93a) while elsewhere angels are described as roasting meat for Adam (bSanh 59b). Humans, through study of the Torah and practice of the commandments, can overcome death, gain eternal life and become divine beings (see, for example, *DeutRab* 7.12). Moses in particular is presented as having been transformed into a divine being (*DeutRab* 11.10). Especially interesting are the citations which related recitation of angelic liturgy with changed status of humans such as in *DeutRab* 2.36. These are impossible to date, but do remind us that transformation via the recitation of angelic liturgy should not be looked at as a "sectarian" theme.

9 This text is found in multiple copies. See the critical edition by Newsom 1985. She argues that, despite the ambiguity of the case, the scales tip in favor of the document not being a product of the sectarian community due to the presence of a copy at Masada and the particular manner in which God's name is recorded (Newsom 1990).

10 For a lengthier description of this text see Janowitz 2001.

11 The text is preserved only in Armenian so we cannot be sure of the Greek. Marcus speculates in his translation that Philo may have used ἀπαθανατίξω (1953: 82).

12 A young girl is declared to be the goddess Hecate, a priestess is said to have oracular powers from the grave, a drowned girl is called a nymph and receives sacrifices, the dead are "equals of the gods" and they are

said to grant release from illness (Lattimore 1962: 102–6). In a Latin epigram Pomptilla in death is merged with the Queen of the Underworld and becomes the goddess Iuno Inferna (G. Coppola 1931).

13 Winston 1979: 276–7.

14 Deification of kings during their lifetime as in the case of the Ptolemies raises issues about Egyptian religious practices, a topic beyond the scope of this chapter.

15 See Nock's shift from first minimalizing the extent to which requests were made of deified emperors to later finding more evidence for it (1972).

16 Price 1987: 71 points to *Atticum* 12.45.2, 13.28.3, 14.14.1 and 14.19.3.

17 *Philippici* 1.13 and 2.110.

18 *ImpPomp* 41.

19 *Atticum* 1.16.13; Lactantius, *DivInst* 1.15,16–20.

20 Funeral of Augustus 56. 34–46, of Pertinax 75. 4–5.

21 Funeral of Septimus Severus 4.2.

22 Fragment 645 Rose.

23 The term was also used in the sense of becoming immortal by being written into history (Polyibus, *His* 6.54.2 and Diodorus Siculus, *Hist* 1.1).

24 For another example of the verb used in relationship to immortalization in foreign religions, see Diodorus Siculus' analysis of Persian religion, where they are said to worship the dove as a means of immortalizing Semiramis (*Hist* 2.20).

25 Plato, *Charm* 156D and Aristotle, *NicEth* 1177b33. A less flattering Greek version of this story circulated: Zalmoxis was Pythagoras' slave and lived secretly in an underground chamber only to emerge and teach about the afterlife. See Hartog 1988: 84–109.

26 On the deification of the Getea, see also Diodorus Siculus, *Hist* 1.94; Arian, *Anab* i.3.2; Lucian, *Scyth* 1.860, *DeorConc* 9.533.

27 A poem written by a contemporary of Augustus refers to the distinct nature of royal souls (Manilius 1.14).

28 Vespasian deified his daughter after her death (Suetonius, *Vesp* 3, *CIL* 5.2829).

29 On Antinous specifically, see Pausanias 8.9.8 and Dio Cassius 69.11.3. For Antinous inscriptions, see IG 4.590 and 14.960–1 and statues, Kraus 1959.

30 On divinization by drowning in the Nile, see Herodotus, *Hist* 2.90. Drowning of certain animals was also understood to separate the divine part from the mortal body. See *PGM* 1.5 and 3.1.

31 The cult was never celebrated in Rome.

32 In the case of Hadrian, the Senate delayed deification for a month. But as power became more and more centralized in the emperor, the role of the Senate was diminished.

33 See M. Smith 1983.

34 The Chaldaean Oracles as reconstructed by Lewy also include a pseudo-burial.

35 See Harnack 1918: 131–5.

36 The term appears twice in this chapter.

37 Riesenfeld 1946.

38 First argued by Lewy 1978 chapter 3 and succinctly described by Stroumsa 1981. For a slightly different view, see Johnston 1992 and 1997.

39 Fr.122,123,138. Cf. Iamblichus's reference to ascent and its relationship to the Chaldaean sacraments (*DeMyst* 3.31).

40 Papyrus 574 of the Bibliotheque Nationale, *PGM* 1V:475–829.

41 Almost identical techniques are used to achieve an ascent in the Nag Hammadi tractate *Marsanes*, where we find the reciting of hymns, angel names, and strings of vowels combined with periods of silence. See Pearson 1984.

42 Evidence of editing includes the female reference at the start of the text followed by the entirely masculine references within the text. Like the ascent in *Hekhalot Rabbati*, discussed below, this ascent also has additions that appear before the ascent and appended instructions for supplemental rituals. An introductory reference to herbs and spices is usually considered an addition. The end of the text includes instructions for a scarab ceremony and for making amulets, with two additional compositions appended.

43 The Hebrew term used is "descent." For Scholem's speculations on this term, which have not been superseded, see 1954: 46ff. and 1965: 20 n.1.

44 The Hebrew text is available in Schäfer 1981: 81–280 and German translation Schäfer 1987–1991 Vol. II. On its redaction, see Schäfer 1988: 63–74 and Gruenwald 1980: 150–173. *Hekhalot Rabbati* is a composite text which is difficult to date. M. Smith dated one of the apocalyptic sections to mid-fourth century, but also argued, following Scholem, that the other sections contained earlier material going back to the first century (1963).

45 For a recent study of this material and its relationship to earlier strains of thought within Judaism, see Elior 1999.

46 The ascent is part of a composite text which combines several series of hymns with Shi'ur Komah material and the main ascent, which is a combination of two ascents (sections 13–22 and 23–25). The text concludes with additional hymns and two appended stories about forgetting learning.

47 Noted by M. Smith 1963.

48 Two other texts associated with the corpus, 2 Enoch 22: 8–10 and 3 Enoch 4–19, include descriptions of transformation accompanied by fasting, changes of clothing, and blessings. These may have been components of ascent/deification rituals at some point.

49 See the discussion of divine names in Chapter 3.
50 Scholem argued that ascent was a foretaste of the heavenly world (1965: 17–18).
51 A modern remnant of this is the practice of standing on one's toes when reciting the formula from Isaiah.
52 Since the Greek word for "holy" was not frequently used in Greco-Roman prayers, its use is seen as evidence of a Jewish origin for the prayer.
53 Pearson 1984: 337 notes that Michael Psellus made reference to Jewish elements already in the tenth century.
54 They mimic the praises spoken by the heavenly powers which appear earlier in the text.
55 Tanhura *Qedoshim* 37.5. See also *PGM* 1.196ff. and 3 Enoch 35.6.
56 See J. Z. Smith 1978b: 62 n. 99.
57 Nock noted the similarities between *Corpus Hermeticum* 11.20–21 and Philo, *LegAll* 3.44 (1950: 77 n. 7).
58 The various tractates do not agree on all the details of deification. The tenth tractate of the *Corpus Hermeticum* argued that deification means the separation of the body from the soul; hence there is no deification while still in the body (*CH* 10.7). While the human mind is capable of uniting humans with the gods (10.23), death still remains a major barrier. Humans are described as gods who die and gods, as immortal humans (10.25).
59 *GenRab* 90.2 and *Sifre Deut* 49 rationalize the material (M. Smith 1958: 479).
60 *InSTheoph* 8, *Philos* 10.33, 10.34 and the discussion in Harnack 1918: 131–5.
61 *Pesiq RabKah* 25. Compare *LamRab* 1.33. See the discussion in Idel 1988: 158ff.

"Even the decent women practice witchcraft": magic and gender in late antiquity

1 See the work of Valerie Knivelson on men accused of witchcraft in eighteenth century Russia (Knivelson, unpublished).
2 Collections of anecdotes about women and magic in rabbinic texts can be found in Meir Bar-Ilan 1993 and Fishbane 1993.
3 On the power of this trope to reshape events see Ilan 1996: 223–4.
4 Noted above in Chapter 1.
5 On shifting attitudes towards the dead see Schmidt 1994.
6 Discussed in Chapter 1.
7 See the discussion in Gordon 1987: 80–2.
8 See Euripides' *Medea* and Sophocles' *Women of Colchis*.
9 On the witches from Thessaly, see Propertius 1.5.4–6 and 3.24.9–10; Lucan, *BelCiv*, 6.413–830; Statius, *Theb* 3.140–46 and 4.504–11;

Martial 9.29.9; and Juvenal 6.610–12. For Thessalonian women who attempt to bring down the moon, see Aristophanes, *Clouds* 749; Plato, *Gorgias* 513a; Horace, *Epodes* 5.46; Propertius 1.1.19; Lucan, *BelCiv* 5.438–506; and Plutarch, *OrDelphi* 12, *deDeOc* 13.

10 In particular, the rabbis adopted a number of Greco-Roman methods for argumentation such as "from the minor to the major" and develop them into a fine art. See Janowitz and Lazarus 1992.

11 This is not, of course, to say that these fluids *are* naturally unclean, only to point out the type of rhetoric used.

12 Cohen 1991 stresses this point.

13 See, for example, Milgrom's classic argument that items are declared unclean due to associations with death and not with daimonic forces as has previously been argued (1991).

14 See Parmentier 1994: 153–67.

15 This is briefly discussed in Chapter 1.

16 Tacitus, *Hist* 5.6 and Josephus, *BJ* 4.480. See also Strabo, *Geo* 16.2.43 who cites Posidonius as an ancient source for this notion and who associates it particularly with Jews.

17 See also the reference to Hypatia using a menstrual rag to avert hail (Damascius, *VitIsid* 77.13f.).

18 Lieberman 1965: 102 n. 51 mentions mNid 7:3.

19 The story is found in mSanh 6:4; the identification of the women as witches in bSanh 45b; jHag 2.2; jSanh 5.9.

20 For example, a woman can turn into a donkey (bSanh 67b).

21 See Ilan 1996: 189 on evidence about midwives in rabbinic literature.

22 See the discussion by Tal Ilan 1997: 86–8. A similar reference to delaying childbirth is found in *Theaetetus* 149C–D.

23 bYoma 84a; jAZ 2.2; and jShab 14.4. In the first version she is anonymous, in the second her name is recorded as "Thimtinis" and in the third "Bat Domitian."

24 Women in patriarchal societies do not have the freedom or resources to start women's religions; social factors such as matrifocality, some emphasis on female lines of descent, or gender dissonance explain the exceptions (Sered 1994, especially p. 64).

25 So, too, Beruriah, the rare figure of an educated female in rabbinic literature, rules on practical issues related to women. Her most interesting traditions are also late (Goodblatt 1975).

Concluding note: the legacy of the first centuries

1 Ha-Aretz newspaper, English edition, 24 June, 1999, p. 2.

BIBLIOGRAPHY

PRIMARY SOURCES

Primary source citations are by standard editions (e.g., Loeb Classical Library), except for the following cases.

Tanhuma

Buber, S. (ed.) (1885) *Midrash Tanhuma,* Vilnius: [s.n.] Reprinted 1946 New York: s.n.

Lamentations Rabba

Bubber, S. (ed.) (1898/99) *Eicha Rabba,* Vilnius: [s.n.]

Sefer Ha-Razim

Margalioth, M. (1966) *Sefer ha-razim*, Jerusalem: Keren Yehudah leb u-Mini Epshtein she-'al yad ha-Akademyah le-Mada'e ha-Yahadut be-Artsot ha-Berit.

Morgan, M.A. (1983) *Sepher ha-razim = The Book of the Mysteries*, Chico, Ca.: Scholars Press.

CII

Frey, J.-B. (ed.) (1963) *Corpus Inscriptionum Iudaicarum,* Rome: Pontificio Instituto.

CIL

Corpus Inscriptionum Latinarum (1862), Berolini: G. Reimer.

Ps-Democritus, Olympiodorus, and Zosimos

Ber = Berthelot, M. and Ruelle, C.-E. (1963) *Collection des anciens alchemistes grecs,* London: Holland Press (reprint).

Gorgias and Xenophanes

DK = Diels, H. and Kranz, W. (1951) *Die Fragmente de Vorsokratiker* (6th edn), Berlin: Weidmann.

PGM

Henrichs, A. (ed.) (1973) *Papyri graecae magicae* (2nd edn), Stuttgart: Teubner.

Proclus
InTim = Diehl, E. (ed.) (1904) *Commentary on the Timeaus,* Leipzig: Teubner.
ThPl = Saffrey, H.D. and Westerink, L.G. (eds and trans.) (1981) *Théologie Platonicienne {Platonic Theology}* Paris: Les Belles Lettres.
InPlatRemp = Kroll, G. (ed.) (1899) *Commentary on Plato's Republic,* Leipzig: Teubner.
InCratyl = Pasquali, G. (ed.) (1908) *Commentary on Cratylus,* Leipzig: Teubner.

Syncellus
Mosshammer, A. (ed.) (1984) *Ecloga Chronogrphia,* Leipzig: Teubner.

SECONDARY SOURCES

Alexander, P.S. (1986) "Incantations and Books of Magic," in G. Vermes, F. Millar and M. Goodman (eds), *The History of the Jewish People in the Time of Jesus Christ* (3rd edn) (pp. 342–79), Edinburgh: Clark.
Annas, J. (1992) *Hellenistic Philosophy of the Mind*, Berkeley: University of California Press.
Austin, J.L. (1962) *How to do Things with Words*, Oxford: Clarendon Press.
Barb, A.A. (1963) "The Survival of Magic Arts," in A. Momigliano (ed.), *The Conflict between Paganism and Christianity in the Fourth Century* (pp. 100–14), Oxford: Oxford University Press.
Bar-Ilan, M. (1993) "Witches in the Bible and in the Talmud," in H. Basser and S. Fishbane (eds), *Approaches to Ancient Judaism,* Vol. 5 (pp. 7–22), Atlanta, Ga: Scholars Press.
Barker, M. (1992) *The Great Angel: A Study of Israel's Second God*, London: SPCK.
Barton, T. (1994) *Ancient Astrology*, London: Routledge.
Berthelot, M. (1885) *Les origines de l'alchimie*, Paris: Steinheil.
—— (1938) *Introduction a l'etude de la chimie, des anciens et du moyen age,* Paris: Steinheil.
Betz, H.D. (ed.) (1986) *The Greek Magical Papyri in Translation, Including the Demotic Spells*, Chicago: University of Chicago Press.
Bickerman, E. (1929) "Die römischen Kaiserapotheose," *Archiv für Religionswissenschaft*, *27*, 1–29.
Bickerman, E. and Smith, M. (1976) *The Ancient History of Western Civilization*, New York: Harper and Row.
Blau, L. (1914) *Das altjüdische Zauberwesen*, Leipzig: L. Lamm.
Boddy, J. (1989) *Wombs and Alien Spirits: Women, Men and the Zar Cult in Northern Sudan*, Madison, Wis: University of Wisconsin Press.
Bokser, B. (1985) "Wonder-working and the Rabbinic Tradition: The Case of Hanina ben Dosa," *Journal for the Study of Judaism*, *16*(1), 42–92.
Bonner, C. (1927) "Traces of Thaumaturgic Technique in the Miracles," *Harvard Theological Review*, *20*, 171–81.

—— (1943) "The Technique of Exorcism," *Harvard Theological Review*, *36*, 39–49.

—— (1946) "Magical Amulets," *Harvard Theological Review*, *39*, 25–53.

—— (1950) *Studies in Magical Amulets*, Ann Arbor: University of Michigan.

Bousset, W. (1979) "Eine jüdische Gebetssammlung im siebenten Buch des apostolischen Konstitutionen," *Religionsgeschichtliche Studien. Aufsätze zur Religionsgeschichte des hellenistischen Zeitalters* (pp. 231–86), Leiden: Brill.

Boyarin, D. (1993) *Carnal Israel*, Berkeley: University of California Press.

Brenk, F.E. (1986) "In the Light of the Moon: Demonology in the Early Imperial Period," in W. Haase (ed.), *Aufstieg und Niedergang der römische Welt* Vol. II 16.3 (pp. 2068–145). Berlin: Walter de Gruyter.

Brooten, B.J. (1982) *Women Leaders in the Ancient Synagogue: Inscriptional Evidence and Background Issues*, Chico, Calif.: Scholars Press.

Brown, P. (1972) "Sorcery, Demons and the Rise of Christianity into the Middle Ages," *Religion and Society in the Age of St Augustine* (pp. 119–46), New York: Harper and Row.

—— (1978) *The Making of Late Antiquity*, Cambridge, Mass.: Harvard University Press.

—— (1998) *Late Antiquity*, Cambridge, Mass.: Harvard University Press.

Burkert, W. (1962) "Goes: Zum griechischen Schamanismus," *Rheinische Museum*, *105*, 36–55.

Burrus, V. (1995) *The Making of a Heretic: Gender, Authority, and the Priscillian Controversy*, Berkeley: University of California Press.

Butterworth, G.W. (1916) "The Deification of Man in Clement of Alexandria," *Journal of Theological Studies*, *17*, 157–69.

Chadwick, H. (ed. and trans.) (1965) *Origen: Contra Celsum*, Cambridge: Cambridge University Press.

—— (1976) *Priscillian of Avila*, Oxford: Clarendon Press.

Cohen, S. (1991) "Menstruants and the Sacred in Judaism and Christianity," in Sarah Pomeroy (ed.), *Women's History and Ancient History* (pp. 273–99), Chapel Hill: University of North Carolina.

Colpe, C. (1978) "Geister," in T. Klauser (ed.), *Reallexikon fur Antike und Christentum,* Vol. 9 (pp. 546–53), Stuttgart: Anton Hiersemann.

Copenhaver, B. (1988) "Hermes Trismegistus, Proclus, and the Question of a Philosophy of Magic in the Renaissance," in Ingrid Merkah and Allen Debus (eds), *Hermeticism and the Renaissance* (pp. 79–110), Washington D.C.: Folger.

Coppola, G. (1931) "L'Heroon di Atila Pomptilla in Cagliari," *Rend. Acc. Lincei*, 7, 388–437.

Corin, E. (1998) "Refiguring the Person: The Dynamics of Affects and Symbols in an African Spirit Possession Cult," in Michael Lambek (ed.), *Bodies and Persons: Comparative Perspectives from Africa and Melansia* (pp. 80–103), Cambridge: Cambridge University Press.

Cumont, F. (1907) "Les Anges du paganisme," *Revue de l'histoire des religions*, *55*, 159–82.

—— (1949) *Lux Perpetua*, Paris: P. Geuthner.

Curtis, E. (1992) "Idol, Idolatry," in D.N. Freedman (ed.), *Anchor Dictionary of the Bible,* Vol. 3 (pp. 376–81), New York: Doubleday.

Dan, J. (1967) "Review of The Book of Secrets," *Tarbits*, *37*, 208–14.

de Jong, A. (1997) *Traditions of the Magi: Zoroastrianism in Greek and Latin Literature*, Leiden: Brill.

Diels, H. (1969) "Die Entdeckung des Alkohols," in W. Burkert (ed.), *Kleine Schriften* (pp. 406–41), Hildesheim: G. Olms Verlag.

Dodds, E.R. (1947) "Theurgy and its Relationship to Neoplatonism," *Journal of Roman Studies*, *37,* 55–69.

Duling, D. (1975) "Solomon, Exorcism and the Son of David," *Harvard Theological Review*, *68*, 235–52.

—— (1985) "The Eleazar Miracle and Solomon's Magical Wisdom in Flavius Josephus' Antiquitates Iudaicae 8.42–9," *Harvard Theological Review*, *78*, 1–25.

Elior, R. (1999) "The Merkavah Tradition and the Emergence of Jewish Mysticism," in A. Oppenheimer (ed.), *Sino-Judaica: Jews and Chinese in Historical Dialogue* (pp. 101–58), Tel Aviv: Tel Aviv University.

Faraone, C. (1991) "The Agonistic Context of Early Greek Binding Spells," in C. Faraone and D. Obbink (eds), *Magika Hiera: Ancient Greek Magic and Religion* (pp. 3–32), Oxford: Oxford University Press.

Faraone, C. and Obbink, D. (1991) *Magika Hiera: Ancient Greek Magic and Religion*, New York: Oxford University Press.

Farnell, L. (1916) "Ino-leukothea," *Journal of Hellenic Studies*, *36*, 36–44.

Festugière, A.J. (1932) *L'Idéal religieux des grecs et l'évangile*, Paris: J. Gabalda.

—— (1939) "Alchymica," *L'Antiquité Classique*, *8*, 71–95.

—— (1950) *La révélation d'Hermes Trismegiste*, Paris: Lecoffre.

Fishbane, S. (1993) "Most Women Engage in Sorcery: An Analysis of Female Sorceresses in the Babylonia Talmud," in H. Basser and S. Fishbane (eds), *Approaches to Ancient Judaism,* Vol. 5 (pp. 143–65), Atlanta, Ga: Scholars Press.

Flint, V. (1991) *The Rise of Magic in Early Medieval Europe,* Princeton, NJ: Princeton University Press.

Forbes, R.J. (1948) *Short History of the Art of Distillation*, Leiden: Brill.

—— (1964) "The Origin of Alchemy," *Studies in Ancient Technology,* Vol. 1, (pp. 125–48), Leiden: Brill.

Frankfurter, D. (1995) "Narrating Power: The Theory and Practice of Magical *Historiola* in Ritual Spells," in M. Meyer and P. Mirecki (eds), *Ancient Magic and Ritual Power* (pp. 457–75), Leiden: Brill.

Freedberg, D. (1989) *The Power of Images: Studies in the History and Theory of Response*, Chicago: University of Chicago Press.

Gager, J. (1992) *Curse Tablets and Binding Spells from the Ancient World*, Oxford: Oxford University Press.

Garrett, S.R. (1989) *The Demise of the Devil: Magic and the Demonic in Luke's Writings*, Minneapolis: Fortress Press.

Geertz, H. (1975) "An Anthropology of Religion and Magic, I," *Journal of Interdisciplinary History*, *6*(1), 71–89.

Geller, M.J. (1977) "Jesus' Theurgic Powers : Parallels in the Talmud and Incantation Bowls," *Journal of Jewish Studies*, *28*, 141–55.

—— (1995) "The Influence of Ancient Mesopotamia on Hellenistic Judaism," in J. Sasson (ed.), *Civilizations of the Ancient Near East*, Vol. 1, (pp. 43–54), New York: Scribner's.

Gill, S. (1981) *Sacred Words: A Study of Navajo Religion and Prayer*, Westport, Conn.: Greenwood Press.

Goldin, J. (1963) "On Honi the Circle-Maker: A Demanding Prayer," *Harvard Theological Review*, *56*(3), 233–7.

—— (1976) "The Magic of Magic and Superstition," in Elizabeth Schussler Fiorenza (ed.), *Aspects of Religious Propaganda in Judaism and Early Christianity* (pp. 115–147), Notre Dame, Ind.: University of Notre Dame Press.

Goodblatt, D. (1975) "The Beruriah Traditions," *Journal of Jewish Studies*, *26*, 68–85.

Goodenough, E. (1963) *Jewish Symbols in the Greco-Roman Period*, New York: Pantheon Books.

Gordon, R. (1979) "The Real and the Imaginary: Production and Religion in the Graeco-Roman World," *Art History*, *2*, 1–34.

—— (1987) "Aelian's Peony: The Location of Magic in Graeco-Roman Tradition," *Comparative Criticism*, *9*, 59–95.

Graf, F. (1997) *Magic in the Ancient World*, Cambridge, Mass.: Harvard University Press.

Green, W.S. (1975) "Palestinian Holy Men: Charismatic Leadership and Rabbinic Tradition," in W. Haase (ed.), *Aufsteig und Niedergang der römischen Welt*, Vol. 2.19.2, 619–47.

Gruenwald, I. (1973) "Knowledge and Vision," *Israel Oriental Studies*, *3*, 63–107.

—— (1980) *Apocalyptic and Merkavah Mysticism*, Leiden: Brill.

Gundel, W. (1950) "Alchemie," in T. Klauser (ed.) *Reallexikon für Antike und Christentum*, Vol. 1, (pp. 240–60), Stuttgart: Hiersemann Verlags.

Hachlili, R. (1988) *Ancient Jewish Art and Archaeology in the Land of Israel*, Leiden: Brill.

Halleux, R. (1981) *Les Alchimistes grecs*, Paris: Les Belles Lettres.

Hammond, D. (1970) "Magic – A Problem of Semantics," *American Anthropologist*, *72*, 1349–56.

Hanks, W.F. (1996) "Exorcism and the Description of Participant Roles," in M. Silverstein and G. Urban (eds), *Natural Histories of Discourse* (pp. 160–200), Chicago: University of Chicago.

Harnack, A. (1918) *Der kirchengeschichtliche Ertrag der exegetischen Arbeiten des Origenes*, Vol. 2, Texte und Untersuchungen zur Geschichte der altchristlichen Literatur 42.3, Leipzig: J. C. Hinrichs.

Hartog, F. (1988) *The Mirror of Herodotus: The Representation of the Other in the Writing of History*, Berkeley: University of California Press.

Hoffman, L. (1996) *Covenant of Blood: Circumcision and Gender in Rabbinic Judaism*, Chicago: University of Chicago.

Honoré, T. (1996) "Iulius Paulus," in S. Hornblower and A. Spawforth (eds), *Oxford Classical Dictionary* (pp. 785–6), Oxford: Oxford University Press.

Hopkins, A.J. (1927) "Transmutations by Color: A Study of Earliest Alchemy," in J. Ruska (ed.), *Studien zur Geschichte der Chemie, Festgabe Edmund P. v. Lippman,* Vol. 9–14, Berlin: Springer.

—— (1934) *Alchemy, Child of Greek Philosophy*, New York: Columbia University Press.

Idel, M. (1988) *Kabbalah: New Perspectives*, New Haven, Co.: Yale University Press.

Ilan, T. (1989) "Notes on the Distribution of Jewish Women's Names in Palestine in the Second Temple and Mishnaic Periods," *Journal of Jewish Studies*, *40*, 186–200.

—— (1996) *Jewish Women in Greco-Roman Palestine*, Peabody, Mass.: Hendrickson.

—— (1997) *Mine and Yours are Hers: Retrieving Women's History from Rabbinic Literature*, Leiden: Brill.

Jackson, H.M. (ed. and trans.) (1978) *Zosimos of Panoplis: On the Letter Omega*, Missoula: Scholars Press.

Janowitz, N. (1989) *The Poetics of Ascent: Theories of Language in a Rabbinic Ascent Text*, Albany, N.Y.: State University of New York.

—— (1991) "Theories of Divine Names in Origen and Pseudo-Dionysius," *History of Religions* (4), 359–372.

—— (2001) *Icons of Power: The Pragmatics of Ritual in Late Antiquity*, University Park, Penn.: Pennslyvania State Press.

Janowitz, N. and Lazarus, A.J. (1992) "Rabbinic Methods of Inference and the Rationality Debate," *Journal of Religion*, *72*(4), 491–511.

Johnston, S. (1992) "Riders in the Sky: Cavalier Gods and Theurgic Salvation in the Second Century AD," *Classical Philology*, *87*, 303–21.

—— (1997) "Rising to the Occasion: Theurgic Ascent in its Cultural Milieu," in P. Schaefer and H. Kippenberg (eds), *Envisioning Magic* (pp. 165–193), Leiden: Brill.

Jung, C.G. (1967) *Alchemical Studies*, Princeton: Princeton University Press.

Kapferer, B. (1979) "Emotion and Feeling in Sinhalese Healing Rites," *Social Analysis*, *1*, 153–76.

Kern-Ulmer, Brigitte (1996) "The Depiction of Magic in Rabbinic Texts: The Rabbinic and the Greek Concept of Magic," *Journal for the Study of Judaism*, *27.3*, 289–303.

Keyser, P.T. (1990) "Alchemy in the Ancient World: From Science to Magic," *Illinois Classical Studies*, *15.2*, 353–72.

Kingsley, P. (1995) "Meetings with Magi: Iranian Themes among the Greeks, from Xanthus of Lydia to Plato's Academy," *Journal of the Royal Asiatic Society*, *n.s. 3*, 165–209.

Kippenberg, H. (1995) "Magic in Roman Civil Discourse: Why Rituals

Could be Illegal," in M. Meyer and P. Mirecki (eds), *Ancient Magic and Ritual Power* (pp. 137–63), Leiden: Brill.

Knivelson, V. (unpublished) "Accusations of Witchcraft Made Again Men in 18th Century Russia."

Knohl, I. (1995) *The Sanctuary of Silence: The Priestly Torah and the Holiness School*, Minneapolis: Fortress Press.

Knox, W. (1930) "Jewish Liturgical Exorcism," *Harvard Theological Review*, *31*, 191–203.

Kohler, K. (1901) "Angelology," in I. Singer (ed.), *Jewish Encyclopedia,* Vol. 1 (pp. 583–97), New York: Ktav.

Kohut, A. (1866) *Über die judische Angelologie und Daemonologie in ihrer Abhangigkeit vom Parsismus*, Leipzig: Brockhaus.

Kotansky, R. (1995) "Greek Exorcistic Amulets," in M. Meyer and P. Mirecki (eds), *Ancient Magic and Ritual Power* (pp. 243–77), Leiden: Brill.

Kraus, T. (1959) "Das Bildnisse des Antinous," *Heidelberger Jahrbücher*, *3*, 48–67.

Krausz, M. (1989) *Relativism: Interpretation and Confrontation*, Notre Dame, Ind.: University of Notre Dame Press.

Kuemmerlin-McLean, J. (1992) "Magic, Old Testament," in D. N. Freedman (ed.), *Anchor Dictionary of the Bible,* Vol. 4 (pp. 467–71), New York: Doubleday.

Langton, E. (1949) *Essentials of Demonology*, London: Epworth Press.

Lattey, C. (1916) "The Deification of Man in Clement of Alexandria: Some Further Notes," *Journal of Theological Studies*, *17*, 257–62.

Lattimore, R. (1962) *Themes in Greek and Latin Epitaphs*, Urbana: University of Illinois.

Lauterbach, J. (1925) "The Ceremony of Breaking a Glass at a Wedding," *Hebrew Union College Annual*, *2*, 351–80.

—— (1936) "Tashlich," *Hebrew Union College Annual*, *11*, 207–340.

Lefkowitz, M. and Fant, M. (1992) *Women's Life in Greece and Rome*, Baltimore: Johns Hopkins University Press.

Levinas, E. (1994) *Nine Talmudic Readings*, Bloomington: Indiana University Press.

Levine, B. (1974) *In the Presence of the Lord*, Leiden: Brill.

Lewy, H. (1893) "Morgenländerischer Aberglaube in der römischen Kaiserzeit," *Zeitschrift des Vereins für Völkskunde*, 3:24–40, 130–43.

—— (1978) *Chaldean Oracles and Theurgy: Mysticism, Magic and Platonism in the Later Roman Empire* (2nd edn), Paris: Etudes Augustiniennes.

Lieberman, S. (1936) *Tosefeth Rishonim: A Commentary Based on Manuscripts of the Tosefta and Works of the Rishonim and Midrashim in Manuscripts and Rare Editions*, Jerusalem: Bamberger et Vahrman.

Lieberman, S. (1955) *Tosefta ki-peshutah*, New York: Makhon me'ir Liv Rabinovits al-yadai Bet ha-midrash le-revanim she-be-Amerika.

—— (1962) *Hellenism in Jewish Palestine*, New York: Jewish Theological Seminary.

—— (1965) *Greek in Jewish Palestine, Studies in the Life and Manners of Jewish Palestine in the II-IV Centuries* CE, New York: P. Feldheim.

—— (1974) "Some Notes on Adjurations in Israel," *Texts and Studies* (pp. 69–74), New York: Ktav.

Lindsay, J. (1970) *The Origins of Alchemy in Graeco-Roman Egypt*, New York: Barnes and Noble.

Linforth, I. (1918) "Hoi Anathanatidzoi," *Classical Philology*, *13*, 22–33.

Lippmann, E.O.v. (1919) *Entstehung und Ausbreitung der Alchemie*, Berlin: Springer.

Luck, G. (1985) *Arcana Mundi: Magic and the Occult in the Greek and Roman Worlds*, Baltimore: Johns Hopkins University Press.

Maier, J. (1968) "Das Buch der Geheimnisse," *Judaica*, *24*, 98–111.

Majercik, R. (1989) *The Chaldean Oracles: Text, Translation, and Commentary*, Leiden: Brill.

Marcus, R. (1953) *Philo*, Cambridge, Mass.: Harvard University Press.

McCown, C.C. (1922) "The Christian Tradition as to the Magical Wisdom of Solomon," *Journal of the Palestine Oriental Society*, *2*, 1–24.

—— (1923) "The Ephesia Grammata in Popular Belief," *Classical Philology*, *54*, 128–40.

Merchavya, C. (1967) "Review of Margalioth's *Sefer Ha-Razim*," *Kiryat Sefer*, *42*, 188–92, 297–303.

Meyer, M. and Mirecki, P. (eds) (1995) *Ancient Magic and Ritual Power*, Leiden: Brill.

Michl, J. (1962) "Engel," in T. Klauser (ed.), *Realexicon für Antike und Christentum*, Vol. 5 (pp. 60–97), Stuttgart: Anton Hiersemann.

Milgrom, J. (1991) *Leviticus*, New York: Doubleday.

Momigliano, A. (1975) *Alien Wisdom: The Limits of Hellenization*, Cambridge: Cambridge University Press.

Moore, C. (1996) *Tobit*, Garden City, NY: Doubleday.

Munck, J. (1967) *The Acts of the Apostles*, Garden City, N.Y.: Doubleday.

Naveh, J. and Shaked, S. (eds) (1985) *Amulets and Magicals Bowls: Aramaic Incantations of Late Antiquity*, Jerusalem: Magnes Press.

—— (eds) (1993) *Magic Spells and Formulae: Aramaic Incantations of Late Antiquity*, Jerusalem: Magnes Press.

Neusner, J. (1969) "The Phenomenon of the Rabbi in Late Antiquity," *Numen*, *19*, 1–20.

—— (1989) "Science and Magic, Miracle and Magic in Formative Judaism: the System and the Difference," in J. Neusner, E.S. Frerichs and P.V.M. Flesher (eds), *Religion, Science, and Magic: in Concert and in Conflict* (pp. 61–81), New York: Oxford University Press.

Neusner, J., Frerichs, E. S. and Flesher, P. V. M. (1989) *Religion, Science, and Magic: in Concert and in Conflict*, New York: Oxford University Press.

Newsom, C. (1985) *Songs of the Sabbath Sacrifice: A Critical Edition*, Atlanta, Ga.: Scholars Press.

—— (1990) " 'Sectually-Explicit' Literature from Qumran," in W. Propp,

B. Halperin and D. N. Freedman (eds), *The Hebrew Bible and its Interpreters* (pp. 167–87), Winona Lake, Ind.: Eisenbrauns.

—— (1992) "Angels," in D.N. Freedman (ed.), *Anchor Dictionary of the Bible*, Vol 1 (pp. 248–53), New York: Doubleday.

Niggemeyer, J.H. (1975) *Beschworungsformeln aus dem 'Buch der Gehemnisse'*, Hildersheim: Georg Olms Verlag.

Nilsson, M. (1946) "The New Conception of the Universe in Late Greek Paganism," *Eranos*, *44*, 20–7.

—— (1948) *Greek Piety*, Oxford: Clarendon Press.

Nock, A.D. (1951) "Review of Meecham's *Epistle to Diognetus*," *Journal of Religion*, *31*, 214–16.

—— (ed. and transl.) (1966) *Sallustius: Concerning the Gods and the Universe*, Hildesheim: Georg Olms.

—— (1972) *Essays on Religion and the Ancient World* (edited by Z. Stewart), Oxford: Clarendon Press.

Nock, A.D. and Festugière, A.J. (1950) *Corpus Hermeticum*, Paris: Les Belles Lettres.

North, J.A. (1975) "Praesens Divus: Review of S.Weinstock's *Divus Julius*," *Journal of Roman Studies*, *65*, 171–7.

Olyan, S. (1993) *A Thousand Thousand Serve Him: Exegesis and the Naming of Angels in Ancient Judaism*, Tübingen: Mohr.

Padel, R. (1983) "Women: Model for Possession by Greek Daemons," in A. Cameron and A. Kuhrt (eds), *Images of Women in Antiquity* (pp. 3–19), Detroit: Wayne State Press.

Parmentier, R.J. (1994) *Signs in Society: Studies in Semiotic Anthropology*, Bloomington: Indiana University Press.

Patai, R. (1994) *The Jewish Alchemists: A History and Source Book*, Princeton, N.J.: Princeton University Press.

Pearson, B. (1981) "Jewish Elements in Corpus Hermeticum I (Poimandres)," in R. Van Den Broek and M. J. Vermassen (eds), *Studies in Gnosticism Presented to Gilles Quispel* (pp. 336–48), Leiden: Brill.

—— (1984) "Gnosticism as Platonism: With Special Reference to Marsanes (NCH 10,1)," *Harvard Theological Review*, 77(1), 55–72.

Perdrizet, P. (1903) "Sphragis Solomonos," *Revue des etudes greques*, *16*, 42–61.

Pfister, F. (1894) "Epode," in A. F. v. Pauly and G. Wissowa (eds), *Paulys Realencyclopädie der classischen Altertumswissenschaft*, Vol. Suppl. 4 (pp. 323–44), Stuttgart: A. Druckenmüller.

Pfister, R. (1935) *Teinture et Alchimie dans l'orient hellenistique*, Praha: Institut Kondakov.

Pharr, C. (1932) "The Interdiction of Magic in Roman Law," *Transactions of the American Philological Association*, *63*, 269–95.

Plessner, M. (1976) "Zosimus," in C. Gillispie (ed.), *Dictionary of Scientific Biography*, Vol. 14 (pp. 631–2), New York: Scribner's.

Pope, M. (1977) *The Song of Songs*, Garden City, N.Y.: Doubleday.

Preisendanz, K. (trans. and ed.) (1931) *Papyri graecae magicae*, Leipzig: Teubner.

Price, S. (1984) "Gods and Emperors: The Greek Language of The Roman Imperial Cult," *Journal of Hellenic Studies*, *104*, 79–95.

—— (1987) "From Noble Funeral to Divine Cult: The Consecration of Roman Emperors," in D. Cannadine and S. Price (eds), *Ritual of Royalty: Power and Ceremonial in Traditional Societies* (pp. 56–105), Cambridge: Cambridge University Press.

Rappe, S. (1995) "Metaphor in Plotinus' *Enneads* v 8.9," *Ancient Philosophy*, *15*, 155–72.

Rawson, E. (1985) *Intellectual Life in the Late Roman Republic*, Baltimore: Johns Hopkins University Press.

Richter, G. (1968) *Engraved Gems of the Greeks and the Etruscans*, London: Phaidon.

Riesenfeld, H. (1946) "Remarques sur les hymnes magiques," *Eranos-Jahrbuch*, *44*, 153–60.

Riess, E. (1893) "Alchemie," A.F. v. Pauly and G. Wissowa (eds), *Paulys Realencyclopädie der Classischen Altertumswissenschaft,* Vol. 1 (pp. 1338–55), Stuttgart: Alfred Druckenmüller.

Riess, E. (1896) "Pliny and Magic," *American Journal of Philology*, *17*, 77–83.

Riley, G.J. (1992) "Demons," in D.N. Freedman (ed.), *Anchor Dictionary of the Bible,* Vol. 2 (pp. 445–55), New York: Doubleday.

Rohde, E. (1901) *Kleine Schriften*, Tübingen: Mohr.

Salzman, M.R. (1987) "Superstitio in the Codex Theodosianus and the Persecution of Pagans," *Vigiliae Christianae*, *41*, 172–88.

Schäfer, P. (1987–91) *Übersetzungen der Hekhalot-Literatur*, Tübingen: Mohr.

—— (1988) "The Problem of the Redactional Identity of Hekhalot Rabbati," in P. Schäfer (ed.), *Hekhalot-Studien* (pp. 63–74), Tübingen: Mohr.

—— (1990) "Jewish Magic Literature in Late Antiquity and Early Modern Ages," *Journal of Jewish Studies*, *41*(1), 75–91.

Schäfer, P., Schlüter, M. and Mutius, H.v. (1981) *Synopse zur Hekhalot-Literatur*, Tübingen: Mohr.

Schmidt, B. (1994) *Israel's Beneficent Dead*, Tübingen: Mohr.

—— (1995) "The 'Witch' of En-dor, 1 Samuel 28, and Ancient Near Eastern Necromancy," in M. Meyer and P. Mirecki (eds), *Ancient Magic and Ritual Power* (pp. 111–30), Leiden: Brill.

Scholem, G. (1954) *Major Trends in Jewish Mysticism* (3rd edn), New York: Schocken Books.

—— (1965) *Jewish Gnosticism, Merkabah Mysticism, and Talmudic Tradition* (2nd edn), New York: Jewish Theological Seminary of America.

Segal, A. (1980) "Heavenly Ascent in Hellenistic Judaism, Early Christianity, and their Environment," in W. Hasse (ed.), *Aufsteig und Niedergang der römischen Welt, II, Principat*, Vol. 23.2 (pp. 1333–94), Berlin: Walter de Gruyter.

Sered, S.S. (1994) *Priestess Mother Sacred Sister: Religions Dominated by Women*, Oxford: Oxford University Press.

Simon, M. (1986) *Verus Israel: A study of the Relations Between Christians and Jews in the Roman Empire (135–425)*, Oxford: Oxford University Press.

Smith, J.Z. (1978a) "Towards Interpreting Demonic Powers in Hellenistic and Roman Antiquity," in W. Hasse (ed.) *Aufstieg und Niedergang der römischen Welt*, Vol. 2.16.1 (pp. 254–394), Berlin: Walter de Gruyter.

—— (1978b) *Map is Not Territory: Studies in the History of Religions*, Leiden: Brill.

—— (1979) "Hellenistic Religions," *The New Encyclopaedia Britannica* (17th edn), Vol. 7 (pp. 788–91), Chicago: Encyclopaedia Britannica.

—— (1995) "Trading Places," in M. Meyer and P. Mirecki (eds), *Ancient Magic and Ritual Power* (pp. 13–27), Leiden: Brill.

Smith, M. (1958) "The Image of God: Notes on the Hellenization of Judaism with Especial Reference to Goodenough's work on Jewish symbols," *Bulletin of the John Rylands Library*, *40*, 473–512.

—— (1963) "Observations on Hekhalot Rabbati," in A. Altmann (ed.), *Biblical and Other Studies* (pp. 142–160), Cambridge: Harvard University Press.

—— (1965) "The Ascent of Simon Magus in Acts 8," *Harry Austryn Wolfson Jubilee Volume* (pp. 735–49), Jerusalem: [s.n.].

—— (1978) *Jesus the Magician*, New York: Harper and Row.

—— (1979) "Relations between Magical Papyri and Magical Gems," *Papyrologica Bruxellensia*, *18*, 129–36.

—— (1981) "Ascent to the Heavens and the Beginning of Christianity," *Eranos Jahrbuch*, *50*, 403–29.

—— (1983) "Transformation by Burial," *Eranos Jahrbuch 52*, 87–112.

—— (1986) "Salvation in the Gospels, Paul, and the Magical Papyri," *Helios*, *13*, 63–74.

—— (1987) *Palestinian Parties and Politics that Shaped the Old Testament*, London: SCM Press.

—— (1990) "Ascent to the Heavens and Deification in 4QMa," in L. Schiffman (ed.), *Archaeology and History in the Dead Sea Scrolls* (pp. 181–8), Sheffield: Sheffield Academic Press.

Smith, W.D. (1965) "So-called Possession in Pre-Christian Greece," *Transactions of the American Philological Association*, *96*, 403–26.

Stern, M. (1984) *Greek and Latin Authors on Jews and Judaism*, Jerusalem: Israel Academy of Sciences and Humanities.

Stroumsa, G. (1981) "Review of *Chaldaean Oracles*," *Numen*, *27*, 167–71; 212–24.

Swartz, M.D. (1990) "Scribal Magic and its Rhetoric – Formal Patterns in Medieval Hebrew and Aramaic Incantation Texts from the Cairo–Genizah," *Harvard Theological Review*, *83*(2), 163–80.

—— (1996) *Scholastic Magic: Ritual and Revelation in Early Jewish Mysticism*, Princeton, N.J.: Princeton University Press.

Tabor, J. (1986) *Things Unutterable: Paul's Ascent to Paradise in its Greco-Roman, Judaic, and Early Christian Contexts*, Lanham, Md: University Press of America.

Talmon, S. (1978) "The Emergence of Institutional Prayer in Judaism in the Light of the Qumran Literature," in M. Delcor (ed.), in *Qumran: Sa piété, sa théologie, et son milieu* (pp. 265–84), Paris: Leuven.

Tambiah, S.J. (1968) "The Magical Power of Words," *Man*, *3*, 175–208.

—— (1985) *Culture, Thought, and Social Action: An Anthropological Perspective*, Cambridge Mass.: Harvard University Press.

—— (1990) *Magic, Science, Religion, and the Scope of Rationality*, New York: Cambridge University Press.

Taylor, F.S. (1930) "A Survey of Greek Alchemy," *Journal of Hellenistic Studies*, *50*(1), 109–39.

—— (1937) "The Origins of Greek Alchemy," *Ambix*, *1*(1), 1–37.

—— (1949) *The Alchemists, Founders of Modern Chemistry*, New York: H. Schuman.

Thee, F.C.R. (1984) *Julius Africanus and the Early Christian View of Magic*, Tübingen: Mohr.

Thomas, K. (1971) *Religion and the Decline of Magic*, New York: Scribner's.

Thraede, K. (1969) "Exorzismus," in T. Klauser (ed.), *Realexicon für Antike und Christentum*, Vol. 7 (pp. 44–117), Stuttgart: Anton Hiersemann.

Trachtenberg, J. (1970) *Jewish Magic and Superstition: A Study in Folk Religion*, New York: Atheneum.

Urbach, E.E. (1975) *The Sages, their Concepts and Beliefs*, Jerusalem: Magnes Press.

Veltri, G. (1998) "The 'Other' Physicians: The Amorites of the Rabbis and the Magi of Pliny," *Korot*, *13*, 37–54.

Vermes, G. (1995) *The Dead Sea Scrolls in English*, London: Penguin.

Vyse, S. (1997) *Believing in Magic: The Psychology of Superstition*, Oxford: Oxford University Press.

Waszink, J. (1954) "Bolos," in T. Klauser (ed.), *Reallexicon für Antike und Christentum*, Vol. 2 (pp. 502–8), Stuttgart: Anton Hiersemann.

Wellman, M. (1893) "Aelius Promotus," in A.F.V. Pauly and G. Wissowa (eds) *Paulys Realencyclopädie der Classischen Altertumswissenschaft*, Vol. 1 (pp. 528), Stuttgart: Alfred Druckmüller Verlag.

—— (1897) "Bolos," in A.F.V. Pauley and G. Wissova (eds), *Pauly Realencyclopädie der Classischen Altertumswissenschaft*, Vol. 3 (pp. 676–7), Stuttgart: Alfred Druckmüller Verlag.

—— (1928) "Die Phusika des Bolos Demokritos und der Magier Anaxilaos aus Larissa," *Abhandlungen der Preussischen Akademie der Wissenschaften*, 7.

Wey, H. (1957) *Die Funktionen der bösen Geister bei den griechischen Apologeten des zweiten Jahrhunerts nach Christus*, Winterthur: Verlag P.G. Keller.

Wilamowitz-Moellendorff, U.v. (1959) *Der Glaude der Hellenen*, Basel: B. Schwabe.

Wilken, R. (1983) *John Chrysostom and the Jews*, Berkeley: University of California Press.

Winston, D. (1979) *Wisdom of Solomon*, New York: Doubleday.

INDEXES

PRIMARY SOURCE INDEX

Old Testament

LXX

New Testament

Dead Sea Scrolls

Apocrypha and Pseudepigrapha

Talmud

Other Rabbinic Sources

*See Primary Source Bibliography for edition cited.

Greco-Roman Sources

*See Primary Source Bibliography

GENERAL INDEX